Talking
Middlesbrough
Volume One

Talking Middlesbrough
Volume One

Author Paul Thompson

Concept and Production David Lane

Published by
Legends Publishing
22 Park Road
Hampton Hill
Middlesex
TW12 1HF

E-mail info@legendspublishing.net
Website www.legendspublishing.net

Copyright 2003 by Paul Thompson

Printed and bound in the United Kingdom

This book is dedicated to my daughter Jessica Thompson, with all my love.

Welcome to Volume One of Talking Middlesbrough. This book looks at Boro's history in the words of the men who made it. Thirteen current and former Boro players describe their life and times at the club. From legends like George Hardwick and Juninho, to unsung heroes like Johnny Spuhler. The players featured also include Stuart Boam, John Hendrie and Alan Peacock, which means every season from 1937-1938 to the present day is covered. Through their stories, the history of football over the last sixty years is revealed. From Wartime football and the post-War boom, the abolition of the maximum wage, new stadia, foreign players and the current wages explosion. In the absence of major trophies, Boro fans have always thought of the club's history in terms of the players; Camsell and Fenton in the pre-Second World War era, Mannion and Hardwick in the post-War years, Clough and Peacock, Maddren and Boam, and most recently, Juninho. In this book a cross section of famous and some not so famous names, describe in detail what playing for Boro meant to them. I hope you enjoy it.

Paul Thompson

1974 – Promotion celebrations as Boro clinch the old Second Division title

Thanks to: Mum, Dad, Lynn, Bob Cox, Andy Smith, Paul Readman, Dave Allan and Jane Sanchez.

Watch out for Volume Two of Talking Middlesbrough which is planned to be published November 2004. News and interview updates will be published on **www.legendspublishing.net** in due course.

To see more of Paul Thompson's Boro related photography visit **www.paulthompsonphotography.co.uk**

Some of these interviews have appeared in the Middlesbrough Supporters South magazine. MSS is a fan club for exiled Boro fans, visit http://mss.org.uk.

Contents

George Hardwick

1949 - George Hardwick leads Middlesbrough out at Charlton Athletic before a 3-0 win

I t's not every day you meet an ex-England captain, let alone England's most successful captain in terms of games won. Played thirteen, won ten, drawn two, lost one. For all his achievements in the game, George Hardwick remains relatively unknown outside his native North East. Despite scoring an own goal within a minute of his Boro debut in 1937, he established himself in the England team during the Second World War; first as left back, then as captain. As Wartime internationals are not recognised in the record books, he remains the only England player to make his international debut as captain. A career high point was captaining the Great Britain team which defeated the Rest of Europe six-two at Hampden Park in 1947. After Boro refused to sell George to Juventus and Chelsea, he eventually left in 1950 for a player- coach's role at Third Division Oldham Athletic. After retiring he coached the US Army in Germany, PSV Eindhoven, and the Dutch national team. He returned to coach the Boro youth team, before becoming Sunderland manager. Having saved the Wearsiders from relegation and guided them to their highest post-War League position he was surprisingly sacked. Hardwick was belatedly granted a joint testimonial with Wilf Mannion in May 1983. Talking to George was a great experience; his enjoyment of the life he's been lucky enough to lead was obvious. His pleasure in recounting his exploits was infectious. I was left wondering why English football was unable to find a greater use for his talents following his playing days.

Going back to your youth, did you grow up a Boro fan?

"Yes I was, in fact my grandfather played for Middlesbrough Ironopolis. He played cricket for Yorkshire as well, he was a hell of a sportsman. My father had a chest problem and could only play cricket."

You had an eventful debut, what happened?

"We played Bolton at home, in the First Division. The ground was icy, they kicked off, made progress down the left flank and played a long ball into our eighteen-yard box. Their number nine and Bob Baxter went for the ball, it glanced off them and landed near the penalty spot.

I was covering with the winger behind me. I thought, do the easy thing and without looking I played it back. Then I heard a noise from the crowd, I looked round and Dave Cumming the keeper was on his hands and knees scrambling after it. [Laughs] He slipped on the icy ground and I can see it now rolling neatly into the far corner. But it gave me something to play for, I had to go like hell after that."

Your team-mates must have had a thing or two to say.

"Bob Baxter was one of the greatest players I ever played with, as well as being a clown. He was a fantastic man. He said, 'Don't worry son, we'll put it right.' I resolved to put it right. I made two breaks, got to the edge of the box, went to the touchline and pulled it back for George Camsell both times. He was one of the greatest goalscorers of all time, and he missed them both [laughs]."

How good was the Boro side you broke into before the War?

"Great. I think Middlesbrough would have won everything had the War not come, because they had so many great players. Bob Baxter was captain of Scotland, Dave Cumming was Scotland's keeper, little Joey Williams on the left wing was a Welsh international and Ralph Birkett on the right wing played for England too. It was a great team, there was a sureness in midfield, and the boss bought well. He bought Duncan McKenzie from Brentford, what a player. With Bill Forrest on the left, what a midfield. And of course, Bob Baxter in the middle, what a hell of a man. He'd win the ball in his own penalty area, and wouldn't move it out 'til he'd had a little play with it. The manager used to say, 'You'll fucking kill me one of these days, my heart won't stand it.' Dave Cumming was an excitable Aberdonian, Baxter would win the ball in the box, and roll it back with his foot. Dave would be shouting, 'BAXTER, BAXTER, GET THAT EFFING BALL AWAY.' And Baxter laughed. I took a lot of leaves out of his book, because I didn't want to give the ball away, I wanted to play. I used to spend a lot of time in the opponents' half, whereas defenders usually were just defenders."

According to the reference books, Boro were never quite as good after the War, why do you think that was?

"We lost people like Bob and Bill Forrest, and the team had to be rebuilt. Wilf Mannion and I came out of the Forces, and there were one or two others who were up and coming. I'd been playing for England all the War years and came home as England captain, but Middlesbrough were always reluctant to spend money. I do honestly believe that had it not been for the War, Middlesbrough would have won everything.

Even after the War they were great entertainment value. Middlesbrough drew record crowds wherever they went because of the quality of the play. We fell down because we didn't have hard men. You always need somebody who's going to bite. We had too many footballers."

Was the decline of the team the reason you wanted to leave?

"During the War I was in the RAF, based down in Kent. I was playing as a guest for Chelsea - in fact I played in two Wartime Cup Finals for them. As soon as I was demobbed I went to Stamford Bridge. The Chelsea chairman and manager, Billy Birrell, an ex-Middlesbrough player, came up here and met the Middlesbrough chairman and manager. I was actually there when the Chelsea chairman put a blank cheque on the desk and told the Middlesbrough secretary to fill it in. But they wouldn't. No way."

It must have been frustrating to be tied to the club.

"Yes, but it was the same for Wilf Mannion, we both could have gone to play in Italy."

That was when Juventus made the joint bid for you and Mannion.

"You just could not leave until such time as they wanted rid of you."

Now with players having much more power, clubs would probably say let's get the best price.

"Yes, even years later when Wilf and I wanted a testimonial game, for some unknown reason, the directors of Middlesbrough would not grant us use of the stadium. God knows how many people wanted to help us, but the chairman and the directors would not bite. I couldn't figure this out because I knew the chairman."

After the War you captained England thirteen times, do any of those games stand out in your memory?

"Oh yes. We used to go on an England tour at the end of every season. One of them was Norway, Sweden, Denmark, then on to the continent. We played Switzerland who weren't exactly a great force in continental football in 1947. But the good Lord ordained that they should beat England one-nil. It was my fault. We'd been playing twenty-five or thirty minutes, and their number nine was playing deep.

Neil Franklin was going with him, and their inside right was breaking through into the gap like a number nine should. I didn't pick him up because I was covering the right winger. But the inside right kept getting through, and he scored. Then it clicked. This is the bloody number nine although he's got an eight on his back, he's the centre forward. I sorted it out, but they'd got the goal lead. For the rest of the game we kicked in. Stan Matthews hit the post but we couldn't rescue the match.

Because we were always winning, the press lads had nothing bad to write about, so they crucified us. [Laughs] From there we went down to Portugal, who were kings of Europe at the time. In the tunnel I turned to the lads and said, 'lets make those bastards up there eat every bloody word they've printed.' We were all growling. Poor old Portugal didn't stand a chance. We were four-nil up in about ten minutes. It finished ten-nil. It was some performance, probably the greatest ever by an England team. Although an eight-two beating of Holland wasn't bad, that was later on at Huddersfield."

This is probably an impossible question to answer, but can you describe the experience of captaining England in front of a hundred thousand plus Scots at Hampden?

"Oh it's great, because I'm of Scottish descent I always wanted to win against Scotland. Particularly against Scotland!"

Did you win at Hampden?

"We licked Scotland six-one on one occasion and had a great team."

A lot of people see the post War years as a golden age of English football, do you agree?

"Yes, the War years were good for football, because you didn't have to bust a gut to win, you played to entertain. Football was followed as if there wasn't a War on. I remember playing for Chelsea, in front of a packed house at Fulham, when the Doodlebug warning went off. It came down just the other side of the water, shaking the stands and everything else. It had become automatic for all Londoners that, as soon as you heard the warning, you should hit the deck. I remember to this day there was silence after the chaos, when I looked up it was as if there was no one there. All the crowd, players, referee and linesmen, all on the deck, some on top of each other. It was one of the funniest things I've ever seen!"

How good was Wartime football?

"Football in the War was played to a very high standard. RAF against the Army games had twenty-two full internationals. When they turned on the style it was tremendous.

All the Scotsmen and Welshmen were in the Army team, and the RAF team was just about the England side at one time. Stan Matthews, Tom Finney, Ted Drake, Neil Franklin, and Bert Williams was our 'keeper."

If you could choose, would you rather play now or when you did?

"When I did."

Even though you earned a pittance?

"Yes, it wasn't so urgent. Although I never ever wanted to lose. I would do anything to win. Wilf wasn't a winner mentally. He could lose and not worry. If I lost, my wife used to get out the back door and run. [Laughs] I was a bad loser. Certainly there were some great players before the War, and some great football played.

But it was a joy to play during the War, because the pressure wasn't on so much. When we came out of the Forces when hostilities ended I carried this attitude and this style into the game, and it gained something. It's a funny thing to say, but I wouldn't have missed the War years, although it frightened the shit out of me at times. [Laughs] Every Christmas Day there are still three phone calls I get from my old mates."

What were the best and worst experiences of your time at Boro?

"The worst was playing Burnley in the Sixth Round of the Cup. We were winning one-nil at Ayresome Park and Micky Fenton scored to make it two-nil with about fifteen minutes to go. But the linesman started waving his flag. The referee went to him and disallowed the goal. He gave Johnny Spuhler offside when he was stood next to the linesman.

How could he have been interfering with play? They scraped a draw and went to Burnley for the replay. The ground was frozen, I've never seen anything like it, before or since. They had people with crowbars chipping out the touchlines and filling them in with sawdust. It was never ever fit to play on.

But I could always manage pretty well under any conditions. We used to get touring parties in the War, as a bit of relaxation for the lads, jugglers and tightrope walkers - it was there I discovered my sense of balance was good enough for me to walk the tightrope.

But we played the game. Nobody looked like scoring, the ball was all over the place, everyone was slipping over. Their winger got past Dicky Robinson and crossed into our box, Dave Cumming came out and

1948 – George Hardwick during England's 2–0 win in Glasgow before 135,000 fans

caught the ball, but as he came down his feet went from under him. He was lying on his back with the ball just by him. I was on the goal line, I can see it now. Their centre forward pushed the ball out with his hand to Johnny Morris, [laughs] the little Welsh bastard, who side-footed it into the net.

It was a bit of a laugh 'til I looked up and saw the referee pointing to the centre spot. Why he didn't send me off, God only knows, I called him everything. I couldn't even get him to go to the linesman. They beat us one-nil and won the Cup. It was our year, we had the right attitude at long last. Unlike Middlesbrough teams who had always been gentle folk, we had Harry Bell who could bite a bit. Wilf didn't like Harry, said he couldn't play, so I asked him if he wanted to go and win the ball instead?

Wilf wasn't a great team man, only on occasions. I remember we went to play at Wolves, and under Major Frank Buckley they always used to soak the pitch. We played ninety minutes, and came off having drawn one-one. I always let the lads go in the bath and had mine later.

I had a chat while I was waiting with Charlie Cole the trainer, big fat bugger, a tremendous character. After the game the trainer had to sort out the kit and put it in the basket, ready for laundering. Only Charlie and I were in the dressing room, all the lads were in the bath. He picked up Wilf's stockings and said, 'there's no point wasting fucking money laundering these.' [Laughs] There wasn't a mark on them."

And the best moment?

"There were so many. Every moment in every team I've ever played in was the best moment. I loved it, I couldn't think of a better life than the one I've had, and still have to a certain extent."

Do you still go and watch Boro?

"Oh yes, what the hell else would I do on a Saturday afternoon?"

Did it feel strange to watch a Boro side play at Wembley in 1998?

"Yes, you're so accustomed to seeing the Arsenals and Spurs, teams like that, then suddenly out comes good old Boro. I was so disappointed with the way they performed on the day against Leicester because we all knew they could do so much better."

Maybe it was the pressure of the occasion?

"It shouldn't have been because they were all internationals bar one or two. Mind you, it wasn't easy playing at Wembley, it was a bit of a skating rink. Nobody is allowed to walk on the grass from one match to another and you've only got to step on it and the sap appears."

Is the story that Wembley drains your energy like nowhere else true?

"To a certain extent. The other thing of course is the marching bands, these guys with their big boots marching up and down, bringing out all the moisture. Consequently for the first twenty-five minutes it was like a skating rink. You did get a lot of injuries, but it was a thrill to be there, so you should roll your sleeves up and enjoy it."

You left Boro to become player-manager at Oldham, from there you worked for the US Army, then went to Holland. How easy did you find the transitions?

"It wasn't much different because I'd captained teams, in fact I captained every team I played for. I don't know why, I never asked for it. I was happy to have the armband, because I was always a bossy bugger. To quote my American friends, 'Man, I had a ball.' A wonderful life with wonderful people."

What happened after you left Oldham?

"I was working with Joe Mercer down at Bisham Abbey, coaching youngsters, when I got a call from Walter Winterbottom to go up to the FA offices. There was a couple of high and mighty people from the US Army there who explained they were having problems in Germany between the GIs and the young Germans. They were fighting and all sorts of things, it really was a flash point.

They couldn't think of a way to rectify the situation, until someone suggested that there should be a common denominator. They decided to give soccer a whirl, and they asked me if I would take on the project. I thought this'll be all right, I'll be the boss again. [Laughs] I had to go to the American Embassy and swear allegiance to the flag, and I got full rank of Colonel. So I toddled off to Stuttgart US Army HQ and started to teach them how to mark out a football pitch."

Really, starting from scratch?

"Yes. There were a lot of troops and a lot of bases in Germany, it was great. I had my own six-seater aircraft, my own three-seater helicopter, car and driver. To cut a long story short, they wanted to create some real excitement for the troops. I suggested a US Army Cup. They had some pretty good players and the GIs picked the game up quickly. Beforehand there was no sport for little guys, all their sports are for big burly buggers. So I called all the coaches in and told them they could pick whichever section they wanted, throughout the US Army. I took the medics, the smallest unit in the Army. We won everything in sight, right through to the final. In front of 27,000 GIs in Mannheim stadium - we won by two goals to nil."

Did you want to win as much as coach as you did when you played?

"I've always wanted to win, even do at home. Mind you I don't always win there. [Laughs]"

What did you do after you finished in Germany?

"I went to Holland as manger of the Dutch national team, then PSV Eindhoven came along and doubled my salary. I was a bloody idiot for coming away from Holland, I'm still mad about it. My sons were very young when I was in charge of the Dutch National team, we lived in The Hague. The eldest lad was ten and the school of languages was there, so it was fine for him, but the youngest had to get on the coach at half past seven in the morning and go to the RAF school in Germany. It was a bit rough for a kid, I was constantly aware of it. Then of course PSV came along, I thought the schooling situation would be better, but on the contrary, it was worse. The RAF school was another twenty miles away."

You've never had the same reputation as a coach in this country that you enjoyed in Europe have you?

"No. I always dreamed when I played. I dreamed of organising a team that had no numbers on their backs, no defined place in the team, they were just footballers. I went to Holland and did that."

You laid the foundations for total football?

"I did just that. It worked like a dream, because they were, and still are so coach minded. If I'd told them to go and jump in the river they would do it without question. They were in the early stages of becoming fully professionalised. A lot were still amateurs, but it was blatantly obvious that they would become a strength in the game eventually. By God, they've had brilliant players, but you see they start with clubs at seven years of age. At PSV we turned out thirty-seven teams every Sunday.

Phillip Otten, who was the world boss of Philips who sponsor PSV, would do anything to put Philips on top of the tree. I could ask him for anything. When I started he asked me what had struck me in the short time I had been there. I said the floodlighting wasn't really up to standard. That was on the Friday. On Monday morning there was six Philips electrical engineers in his private aircraft. They flew to the States, from there to Japan, on to Italy and back. Then they went to work. When they'd finished you could see to pick a pin up, literally. That was Phillip Otten.

When I was there we thought we'd signed Ferenc Puskas. He lived with me while we were trying to buy him, but Real Madrid nipped in and bought him - they were at their peak then so he decided to go purely for the appeal of the big time. Of course Ferenc played for Real for a number of years, but I thought we'd got him. When we had him living with us I thought we'd nailed him."

Did you enjoy managing Sunderland?

"Yes, but I'm still not happy about what happened at the end, because I'd done everything to acquire a long term contract. I'd just come back from Holland, I was working for an oil company and as a journalist.

I was in the Sunderland press room after a game, when the secretary asked me to go and see the chairman and directors in the directors' room. I thought I was going to get an exclusive. The chairman said, 'George, you've got experience in management...' I was offered the job. The deal as I understood it was that if I kept them in the First Division, which I did, then we would agree a long term deal. Instead they dispensed with my services at the end of that season."

Is there one thing in your career that you're most proud of?

"Captaining the team that represented Great Britain against The Rest of Europe. I really got a kick out of that. In fact I had a bad knee and wasn't fit to play, but there was no way I was going to miss that one.

I was playing in a team that was good enough to carry me. Walter Winterbottom, who was the manager, said the team were all strangers and I was the only one who could guide them."

What was the score?

"We won six-one, Wilf Mannion got two."

How did you feel about Boro leaving Ayresome Park?

"Before the event I was really uptight about it. I was aware that the adjoining hospital was going to be destroyed, so I thought Boro would use that land. For old times sake, on the Sunday before they auctioned every-thing, my wife Jennifer and I walked round the stadium.

I walked to the spot on the New Stand, as it was known, and there was always a guy there with a voice which boomed. I used to like to fiddle with the ball, I wanted to be a centre forward really. This voice would shout, 'GET RID OF THE EFFING BALL, HARDWICK, GET THAT EFFING BALL AWAY!' I used to get this every match, if I started doing tricks. Wilf always had his hair hanging down, and this guy used to shout, 'GET YOUR EFFING HAIR CUT, MANNION!' They were great days, especially when you won."

The last game at Ayresome Park must have been very emotional for you?

"It was, it was. I had hoped like hell when the news of the hospital closure came through, that the necessity for Boro to leave the site would

1947 – George Hardwick [right] captains Great Britain against The Rest of Europe

be removed. But when I walked round that Sunday, I realised that if they hadn't moved, it would have fallen down - it was finished.

The toilets were a disgrace, and as for the dressing rooms, dear-oh-dear. Thinking of those changing rooms reminds me of Charlie Cole our trainer and how mean the club was. They used to buy slabs of carbolic soap and he used to cut slivers off. As you went into the bath he gave you a shaving of soap, that was it.

And that bath! Wilf used to get a rough time from Bob Baxter, he didn't jump when Baxter told him to. One time Baxter was lying on the massage table naked, and he told Wilf to get powder. There was a big container of it in the dressing room. Wilf took it over to the table, Baxter raised his legs and said, 'my arse is kinda firey, powder my arse.'

So Wilf powders, and powders. Suddenly Baxter farted and Wilf disappeared in a cloud of powder. Wilf then made the fatal mistake of turning on Baxter, and saying in his cultured South Bank tones, 'you dirty cunt, Baxter.' Baxter and Billy Forrest then grabbed Wilf, who was fully clothed and chucked him in the cold bath. He went home in his tracksuit. I used to come away from that place with a bellyache; not from the exertion, from the laughter.

I recall another occasion when all the young players were punished. Ayresome Park and the training area were under inches of snow, so the players were sent off running and our route took us past a church and a farm. The senior players were in front of us and we couldn't resist the fun of blasting them with snowballs. They disappeared round the corner adjoining the church and farm and without thinking we followed them round the corner to find they were waiting just out of sight.

They stripped us naked and set off back to the stadium with our tracksuits and everything else. Thank goodness there was a barn to house twelve young, naked, up and coming footballers. We were stuck there for around an hour until Charlie Cole arrived on his bike with our training gear.

There was no chance of a young player becoming conceited, trainees had to prefix all the big names at the club with 'mister'. But the life of fun and laughter was worth a fortune. All for £8 a week, through £12 and £15 a week, with an additional £2 win and £1 draw bonus. How about that?"

Stuart Boam

Stuart Boam lifts the Anglo-Scottish Cup at Craven Cottage after the 1-0 aggregate win

Stuart Boam was one of my boyhood heroes. My first full season watching Boro was 1973-1974 when they won the old Second Division by fifteen points. I quickly got used to watching Jack Charlton's team demolish all-comers. Had I known then, that Boro's previous promotion to the top flight was in 1929, during the days of George Camsell, I might have appreciated it a bit more. Stuart Boam signed in 1971 from Mansfield and made his debut on the same day as Nobby Stiles. He was a tough, hard tackling centre half, and won player of the year in his first and last season, but it is as captain of the 1973-74 team that people remember him. His partnership with Willie Madden was the rock upon which the rest of the team was built. As well as helping establish Boro in the First Division, he played in the famous cup games of his era, the quarter-finals against Birmingham in 1975, and Orient in 1978. He left for Newcastle in 1979 when Irving Nattrass went the other way. It was a pleasure to meet him, and even more of a pleasure to hear the inside story of one of Boro's best ever teams.

Were you always determined to become a footballer?

"Yes, I played for my school, my district, then my county, and although I went to grammar school, I spent most of my evenings playing football. From the age of eleven I captained every team I played for, including twenty years as a pro, from sixteen to thirty-six."

After starting your career at Mansfield, Stan Anderson signed you for Boro in 1971.

"Stan bought me, but within two seasons we had a new manager, a new chairman, and a new captain, in Jack Charlton, Charles Amer and me. I didn't put my name forward, it could have been Willie Maddren or Graeme Souness instead of myself. I was asked to do it and it paid off, but Willie possibly should have got the honour ahead of me. He did everything else at Middlesbrough Football Club, including sweep the stands. I was rooming with him at the time and it broke his heart when they gave it to me.

Willie's not one for shouting at people, that's probably why Jack gave me the nod. You'll never meet a better bloke. He was so unlucky to have a shortened career, when you consider the ability he had, and then to get Motor Neurone disease. It's not fair, but life's not fair.

I was more physical, but he was quicker. He could tackle, kick with both feet and was great in the air. If anything came into the box it was mine. My job was to get weighed in, but Willie could do it fairly. I never saw him deliberately foul anyone, he was so good, he didn't need to. If he fouled anyone he'd say sorry, I never did.

How we developed the understanding we had, I don't know. We never had time to work at it, because I never used to see him 'til Thursday. He was always on the treatment table - after games his knee would blow up like a football, he'd be in for treatment two or three times a day. Thursday or Friday he'd turn up for tactical work or free kicks, which didn't involve running around, then on Saturdays he'd play. You or I wouldn't walk down the street with a knee that bad, but had it not been for that knee, he would probably have moved onto a bigger a club and got England caps."

Were you bought to play alongside Willie, or was it just something that was tried and found to work?

"My first partner was Bill Gates, but it didn't really work because we were similar players. After Stan Anderson left, Harold Shepherdson was caretaker for eight games and I played alongside Willie in those matches. Then Jack came in."

What do you remember about Jack Charlton's arrival?

"He'd been watching us for several games before he arrived. He took us all up to the Marton Country Club and spoke to us. He went through what he thought of every individual player. When he got to me he said I was crap - his exact words were 'You're crap! Willie Maddren's doing your work for you.' He pulled me to pieces in front of everyone. I thought 'this doesn't seem quite right.' It was probably a wind up, I don't know, he may have meant it.

Willie and I had been playing together for a while, it was the start of a partnership which lasted all Willie's career and most of mine. He slaughtered me, I couldn't head a ball, I couldn't tackle. I've never felt so sick in all my life. Don't get me wrong, Jack and I got on great, but we argued almost every day. He wanted the best for the club, I wanted the best for the players, but we never fell out.

He's still the same now as he was twenty-five years ago. We used to give him a lot of stick about his gear. He'd have soup down his lapel, toast on his tie - he was a right mess at times!

He was with us for four years and he still couldn't remember our players' names, never mind the opposition's. But his training and coaching were brilliant - he organised us. Once that was done we saw less of him. He'd be shooting on a Wednesday and all the apprentices would go missing because he'd have them beating for grouse at his farm.

Thursday he'd be there for payday, Friday he'd put the team sheet up, and if he felt like it he'd turn up on Saturday. [Laughs] But it worked. He had a great system and he got the players to fit it."

Was that the difference between Stan Anderson and Jack Charlton, that Jack had a system?
"Everything was in place at the club when Jack came, his job was to mould it together. You'll never get a better formation than the one we had. You had a defence and a 'keeper who never let any goals in; David Armstrong, Graeme Souness, Alan Foggon and Bobby Murdoch; a fabulous blend of players.

Murdoch and Souness were suppliers, Armstrong and Foggon were the runners. Foggon was grossly overweight, but the fastest man at the club. Jack used to flog him to death in training. The class was Willie Maddren and Souness.

But Foggon breaking from midfield was our trump card. John Hickton and David Mills would make runs and create holes for Armstrong and Foggon to run into. Everywhere Jack's been he's used the same system. Even with Ireland he wasn't bothered about the strikers. He'd have people who could hold it up and make holes for midfield players to run into."

Having told everyone you were crap, did he tell you what you should be doing?

"No. Jack came in as player-manager and I thought I was on the way out. But I kept him out of the team, he didn't play one game. I was the biggest lad so I think he was picking on me to prove a point. He's never told me if he meant it, he just laughs."

The thing people criticise him for now is not spending money on a striker, is that fair?

"We held our own in the old First Division, but we wanted to win something. Had he spent more money, who knows? The players he bought weren't good enough, with respect, like Phil Boersma and Alf Wood. Bobby Murdoch was the best player he bought but he cost nothing. He was tight enough with his own money, never mind the club's. I've seen him climb over the fence at the training ground, knock on somebody's door, then ask for a fag. [Laughs] It all helped to build team spirit though."

How has the game changed in the last twenty-five years?

"The major difference now is that television is running the game. We used to try to stop cameras coming to games because we thought it would knock ten thousand off the gate. Now clubs have to play wherever and whenever they're told."

Do you like the less physical game we have now?

"I still love football. The difference now is it's all one-touch. There was a lot more tackling twenty-five years ago because more players took opponents on - Rodney Marsh, Tony Currie, Trevor Francis, they all took players on. Beckham is the best player England have got, but he doesn't beat people. Jack used to coach Alan Foggon to beat people. His theory was that if you beat a man, you've got the better of him and they're then only playing with nine outfield players. Rodney Marsh only used to play twenty minutes for Q.P.R. in most games - but it was enough.

I remember giving two penalties away against Rodney Marsh, then he sat on the ball to take the piss. He wanted me to welly him. I could have killed him, but he was class. Even keepers now have to kick with both feet, and control the ball. If Platty [Jim Platt] had ever tried to dribble the ball out of his box Jack would have shot him.

It was more physical but I was never sent off in twenty years; now I would have enough points for a suspension and two weeks off over Christmas. I got so many bookings I had my own seat at Lancaster Gate! But I knew where to stop. Once I'd whacked someone that was it. I had the reputation of being harder than I was because Willie was the skilful one, I

was always getting my nose broken, I wasn't born with this thing! I'd come off covered in mud, breathing it in, Willie's kit would be spotless. My motto was 'Thou Shall Not Pass!' I was the same in training, we always finished off with five-a-side, no matter how knackered you were and coach Jimmy Greenhalgh used to give Mars Bars to the winners.

Men on £450 a week, a lot of money then, but they would kill to win. I've seen Souness take people out chest high for a Mars Bar. We all shared the same bath afterwards and if you were last one in you could walk on the water. Forty of us in the bath, five eating Mars Bars! But it was all good for team spirit."

Did you have a blacklist of players you'd played against?

"Not like Jack did. Jack got into a lot of trouble with the authorities because of his little black book. He told me who was in it, but I'm sworn to secrecy. But it was all players who went over the top - that's the worst tackle in the game. It's quite often defenders who get done, because you're clearing the ball, they come in late over the top, there's nothing you can do - it's horrible.

I can honestly say I never went over the top to anyone - intentionally or otherwise. I couldn't ruin a man's career, it's the cowards that do it and once some players start to get a reputation, they do it all the time because they're worried that the next tackle will be someone doing it to them. Referees don't see it. But to answer your question, yes I had a blacklist of sorts, but it wasn't written down."

You hardly missed a game in eight years, did you not get injuries?

"I used to play with them. We went to Ipswich once, I think they were second in the league. We had a warm up on the morning of the game where I was doing some heading practice with Jimmy Headridge and I ricked my neck. It was so bad I couldn't move it at all.

We had no replacement centre-half so my room-mate Willie fetched Jimmy Greenhalgh and we decided not to tell Jack. I sat in the team meeting looking straight ahead and didn't head a ball all afternoon - Willie did it all for me. [Laughs] We got a draw and I got Man of the Match for being so dominant in the air!"

How did the move to Newcastle happen?

"Irving Nattrass had been bought from Newcastle for a big fee, £475,000. The club didn't have much money, so to finance the deal, they sold me to Newcastle. I didn't want to go, in fact I begged not to go. I had meetings with chairman, Charles Amer, because I was only a couple of years away from a testimonial. But I had a good couple of years there."

Was Newcastle a good club at the time?

"It was a club that was run by the players. They'd just got rid of a manager called Richard Dinnis who'd been appointed from coach because the players liked him. Bill McGarry had taken over and he wanted someone to keep them in line."

What happened when you went back to Mansfield?

"After two years at Newcastle, I went back to Mansfield to play. But they wanted me to manage as well. It didn't go well. I'm not making excuses, we were crap. We were in eighth position when I got the sack, having just avoided relegation the previous year, but I'd had enough. There was a clearout of all the expensive players when I arrived. I went there with serious back problems, I had three prolapsed discs. When I did play we did all right. But I needed someone like me to play at the back and I couldn't find anyone. I couldn't improve what we had and I couldn't buy the class I wanted - I was making do with has-beens and never-were's.

I got the sack in the end, it was the best thing that ever happened to me. I was so depressed because it was my hometown, in fact I'm still there. They don't remember what else I did in my twenty-year career, they remember six months here, when it didn't go right, but when I go back to Middlesbrough I'm a hero, people still know me. Even people who never saw me play. After I left Mansfield we went on holiday and I decided I'd had enough. I miss the game sometimes, but I did it for the family. I've got three daughters and I'm not one for moving them around. I built my own house and we're still here. After I built the house I went to work for Kodak, I was there for twelve years. I was in total darkness making films, but it was boring. I was getting nowhere with regards to promotion, but I got maximum redundancy and put it into buying a business."

What's the business?

"It's a newsagents and convenience store. It's long hours, but it's easier now I've got one of my daughters and her boyfriend helping out."

Do you get to many Boro games?

"I get up to see Middlesbrough occasionally and I'm very well looked after. I was there for Willie Maddren's funeral, and before he died, we had reunions several times a year for Motor Neurone Disease fundraising. It was always good to meet the lads again and raise some money. For seven years Willie was probably my best friend as well as my workmate."

What do you think of the wages players get now?

"People say to me, don't you wish you were playing now? Yes I do, but

my legs don't. It was great when I played, different but great, for the time I was well paid too. I was one of the few to have a sponsored car but even the next door neighbour's cat has one now. It made me laugh reading about Ravanelli having his bills paid and so on. If I'd asked Jack to help pay my gas bill he would have cut my head off. [Laughs]"

You won the Anglo-Scottish Cup, how much does that mean to you?

"[Laughs]That was a big competition wasn't it! There was only us and a couple of others in it!"

There's a picture of you being presented with a cup that's about two inches high.

"Bob Lord presented it to me and he hated my guts - he was on the disciplinary committee at the FA. I was up before them once, expecting a three-match ban, but they gave me four. Strangely, the fourth match was against Burnley - Bob Lord was chairman of Burnley. I appealed, which put the ban back and I played against them anyway - and we won. But the Anglo-Scottish was a nothing event."

You also played in the FA Cup Quarter-Final defeats of the time, Birmingham in 1975 and Leyton Orient in 1978.

"I could talk about Birmingham all night. It's well known that we went there and beat them three-nil on the first game of the season. We hammered them at home as well. We should have won the Cup that year, but that's football. Hicky let Bob Hatton run at a corner, the ball hit his head and flew in the corner and Birmingham won one-nil."

People now tend to say Jack was at fault because he went there for a draw.

"We didn't. We ended up playing for a draw because they were on top. They were having a right go because they didn't want a replay. It wasn't our day, things weren't happening for us, so you start to think 0-0 will do. Then they scored with twenty minutes left. Willie and I went up front, but it wouldn't go in - but that's football.

The only time Jack ever sent us out for a draw was against Luton, late in the 1973-74 season, we had about eight games left and were top - Luton were second. A draw at Luton meant we could win the Championship at home the following week and Jack wanted us to do it at Ayresome Park, so he said a draw would do. At half time it was 0-0 everything going to plan and Jack told us to keep it tight. But late in the game, Millsy mis-hit one and it flew into the top corner. At full time we did a lap round the pitch, the home fans were chucking bottles and coins at us. Jack called us in and went ape-shit, because we'd won. [Laughs] Tea cups were flying. 'Everyone sit down, don't fucking move. 'Where is he?' Jack was saying, but Millsy had locked himself in the toilet. [Laughs] Jack would have killed him and we had to sneak him onto the bus. That was the only time I've had a bollocking for winning away from home!

It was funny, but you didn't laugh in front of Jack. I've had jaw-ache from trying not to laugh. We had a team meeting before one game and the team we were playing had a centre forward who'd scored six the week before. Jack sat us down and said, 'Nothing to worry about, five of them were flukes.' I looked at Craggsy and Millsy and they'd gone, but they didn't dare laugh. I couldn't look at anyone, they were all holding it in. When he went we all cracked up. Players, coaches, everyone. I was in pain from laughing."

What's the highlight of your career?

"That season we won the league. It was a great year, nothing went wrong. But I enjoyed my whole time at Middlesbrough."

Robbie Mustoe

Players like Robbie Mustoe are increasingly rare in the game. His twelve years at Boro saw three promotions, two relegations, and three Cup Finals. He signed on the same day as John Hendrie in the summer of 1990 and played under Colin Todd, Lennie Lawrence, Bryan Robson and Steve McLaren. An often unsung hero, he was thought by many to be on borrowed time when Bryan Robson was appointed manager in 1994. Despite many big-name signings Robbie's name remained on the teamsheet throughout Robson's reign. In Nigel Pearson's absence he captained Boro in the F.A. Cup Semi-Final, against Chesterfield in 1997. Sadly, injury meant his appearance in the final was minimal. He also played a full part in the run to the Coca Cola Cup Final that season. Following relegation he was again prominent as Boro again reached the Coca Cola Cup Final and were promoted back to the Premiership at the first attempt in 1998. He shared the fans' player of the season award for 1998-1999, was awarded a well deserved testimonial season in 1999-2000; and went on to play for another two seasons. His finest hour was thought by many to be a magnificent performance in Boro's unlucky defeat to Arsenal in the 2002 F.A. Cup Semi Final. He left the club at the end of the 2001-2002 season.

Did you take much persuading to sign for Middlesbrough?

"No, the deal was done in about twenty minutes."

For quite a sizeable fee for Boro at the time.

"Yes, £375,000. That summer they signed me, John Hendrie for £500,000 and John Wark for just £50,000. We had a decent season, finished in the play-offs where we lost to Notts County. Then Colin Todd got the boot. Considering Boro just avoided relegation the previous season I thought that was harsh."

How did you rate Colin Todd's successor, Lennie Lawrence?

"He was a brilliant talker, a good motivator, and a good man manager. I didn't think his coaching was quite as good as Toddy's, but he made up for it in other ways. They were both good people to work for."

How do Lennie Lawrence and Bryan Robson differ as managers?

"Bryan Robson is always going to have the respect of the players for what he achieved in the game, whereas Lennie never played. We had bad times, but never once did I hear any of the players disillusioned with him. The respect is always there.

Possibly Lennie was a better talker. I've been to a supporters' club meeting with Lennie when we were having a terrible time. The meeting was hostile, but he was brilliant. In the end he got a standing ovation."

In your time at the club the infrastructure changed beyond all recognition. Did the way you train and prepare for games change to the same extent?

"Every manager has his own way of doing things. Our training and preparation didn't change a great deal under Bryan Robson. Training was always enjoyable, with lots of five-a-sides to keep the lads sharp and in good condition for Saturday. Other managers training might be more tactical and team play based, which can bore players."

How important are tactics, and how much is down to players?

"Tactics and systems are important, but if players aren't prepared to work hard you've got a problem. Everybody has to work for each other. That's probably more important than tactics."

What was the difference, if any, between playing with Andy Peake, Jamie Pollock and Jimmy Phillips, and Paul Ince, Juninho and Christian Ziege?

"I enjoyed playing with all those players. Juninho's different. Pollock, Peake, Ince, myself, Maddison, Summerbell, were all hard working players, but with good ability. People would probably say Maddison, Summerbell and myself are getters, but to play at the top level for a period of time you've got to have a bit more in your locker than running around kicking people.

I've played with a lot of midfield players, but in the mould of hard working box-to-box players, Ince is different class. He's what I'd like to be. He tackles, passes the ball, and scores. Bryan Robson did all those things brilliantly too."

Does the raised expectations of the fans put more pressure on the players?

" Yes it does. Their season ticket support has been unbelievable. Unlike Sunderland for example where they've also sold a lot of season tickets, we've invested in big name players on big contracts. So the fans are seeing their money going into the team. This means they expect success. They have every right to expect that things should progress. But money doesn't always bring success immediately.

I think fans expected more of us, but the last time we were promoted again we had a good first season up, then we went down. After promotion we finished ninth, and invested in Ziege and Ince. So the fans were thinking in terms of Europe.

We always aimed to finish higher than the previous season, or considered it an under-achievement. Nobody is complacent, but if you think where Boro were as a club five or so years ago, they're building stability. Every fan must want Boro to be an established Premiership club."

We were three minutes from winning a Cup final and playing in Europe, then had it taken away. Can you understand some fans' impatience?

"That was an unbelievable season. We were poor in the League. The three points the club had deducted for the Blackburn Rovers 'no-show' killed us in the end. But the cups were great.

It was hard to take, but as a player I've got great memories of those games. I'm sure the fans have as well. I was captain for the Chesterfield semi-final, so walking out into the atmosphere at Old Trafford was absolutely fantastic."

Is that the one game you'll tell your grandchildren about?

"It's one of them, along with the Cup Finals. Certainly the first one, that was a huge game. Then you follow it with an FA Cup Final and you realise how little the League Cup really means.

Although I didn't last long due to a torn cartilage. The high spot of my career was probably walking out to play in the FA Cup Final."

Was there really a big bust up between the players on the morning of the FA Cup Final?

"Before the final there had been stories in the papers saying the big names were going to go. Whether they'd actually said that I don't know. Nigel Cox wrote a piece in one of the papers saying that if they weren't staying, why should they be involved in the Cup Final.

Probably a lot of players were thinking the same way. We'd already been relegated and it would be left to the same old blokes to pick up the pieces and get us out of the First Division. This story came out on Cup Final morning and Ravanelli got hold of it. We were having a team photograph at our hotel, in our suits, and Ravanelli was trying to get across to the lads and have a go at Coxy. [Laughs] There were no fisticuffs, but it wasn't in a particularly good spirit considering most of the lads were about to play the biggest game of their careers."

From the players' point of view, which is the most important of the changes in the game over the last ten years?

"Although it took a couple of disasters, and the Taylor Report, the new stadiums are great. It's nice as a player to go to new stadia. Some of the places we went to on the cup runs, or in the First Division were shocking. I know people were unhappy about leaving Ayresome Park with all its memories, but it's great to walk out of the tunnel and see 35,000 cheering fans. The atmosphere here for some of the cup games, like the Liverpool semi final, was fantastic."

You're known as an honest player, but is there more diving and play acting now than when you started?

"Yes, you don't need to be a brain surgeon to see that. It doesn't particularly anger me though, it's part and parcel of football. You have to be very careful in the box as a defending player. Any sort of challenge, whether you get the ball or not the player is going to go over. It's almost at the point now where you can't make a challenge unless you're sure you'll win 100% of the ball. If you foul it's likely to be a booking. The difference between a foul and a booking is getting smaller and smaller."

Do you think referees who have played the game would be able to tell the difference between the fouls and dives?

"It would help, but it's very hard. I sometimes watch games on Sky, and it's only when you see the slow motion that you know what really happened. Where ex-players would help is the cynical nasty foul; like the over-the-top tackle, that referees don't clamp down on. If somebody comes over the ball two-footed he knows what he's doing. I've seen a lot of players get away with that, because they're clever enough to make sure it doesn't look as bad as it is. But I wouldn't want to be a referee."

What's your biggest highlight from your time at Middlesbrough?

"Playing in an FA Cup Final after leading the team out in the Semi-Final at Old Trafford. That season holds a lot of my best memories along with the worst - relegation at the end of it all."

Apart from relegation, is there one major disappointment?

"No major disappointments career-wise. On the pitch the first Cup Final; being three minutes away from winning a trophy. That was the focus throughout those cup runs, to become the first players to win a major trophy for the club. To have that taken away when we were so close to achieving our goal was shocking. Relegation was an awful feeling too.

After the amount of games we'd played we were exhausted. We were playing Saturday, Monday, Thursday, Sunday I think it was. We tried our best and had a decent run right at the end, but the three deducted points killed us. But to be fair to the lads, we bounced straight back. A lot of teams get relegated and don't come back. It was pleasing to prove that we are better than First Division."

What do you say to people who believe all Premiership players are on £50k a week and testimonials are irrelevant?

"People know that only a small percentage of players are on anywhere near that. I've had a good ten years here and made a decent living. I appreciate that. Some people have said to me that they don't think players should have testimonials with the money they earn, but it depends what sort of players you want at your club. If you don't care about loyalty you'll get players like Ravanelli who come for the big money.

When things don't go their way, they leave, then you end up with a team of players who are there for the short-term, and don't give a monkey's for the club, the area, or the fans. Compared to the man in the street, I've earned brilliant money for the last few years. But at thirty-five I couldn't be putting my feet up for the rest of my life. When you stay at a club for a length of time you do get left behind financially, because when players move the salary tends to jump up. Not that I'm complaining, but it's nice to have loyalty recognised. The supporters club and the disabled supporters club both gave me engraved gifts for ten years service. I'm not bullshitting when I say they mean as much as earning x-amount at a dinner. Given the choice of three or four moves, and twice as much money, I wouldn't do anything different."

Ronnie Dicks

Ronnie Dicks was the ultimate utility player. In a fifteen year career he played for Boro in all eleven positions, having filled in as goalkeeper for the injured Rolando Ugolini in 1954. Dicks, a Londoner, came to Teesside during the Second World War. He was posted to an Artillery training camp at Marske in 1943. He signed professional forms for Boro and played wartime football, before seeing active service in Burma. After the war he intended to return to London, to play for a team in the capital. However signing for Boro meant he was tied to the club unless they decided to release him. He returned to Teesside and the Boro first team, and was a regular until his retirement in 1958. In 1950 injury prevented him playing for a Football League representative team, and the England B team. Dicks played in what is now seen as the golden age of English football. Record crowds watched players like Stanley Matthews, Nat Lofthouse, Tom Finney, and of course Wilf Mannion. His memory and opinions were clear and focused. It was fascinating to hear tales of playing with Mannion and Hardwick, and against Matthews. The contrast between people like Ronnie Dicks and modern players shows how revolutionary the recent changes to the game have been.

How did you come to Teesside originally?

"It was a Wartime posting. After preliminary training we were told where we would be going. Most of us were Southerners, so the first question was, 'where the hell is Middlesbrough?' I knew of the football team of course, but I didn't know where Middlesbrough was. I finished up at Marske, at the Artillery barracks."

What where your first impressions of Teesside?

"It was pretty grim and drab. But getting out into the countryside was great. In London you can go miles and miles and not see any countryside. Being in the Artillery we did all our exercises out on the moors. I really liked the wide open spaces."

Did you see active service?

"I was in Africa then Burma, in a division with Africans. There was some very heavy fighting in Burma. The Japs had broken through Singapore into Burma, and the fighting was almost hand-to-hand. There were two famous battles, Imphal, and Kohima. At Imphal they were practically fighting over a tennis court. The Japs ran out of materials, they'd come so far and their supply lines were so extended, that they couldn't keep going. Mountbatten pulled out the Europeans who had done all the fighting and put the Africans in just to hold them, but the Africans kept pushing them back and back. We fought for about three months. Then when the Europeans were ready, they took over again."

What was the standard of the Wartime football you played in?

"It wasn't bad. When I first signed for Middlesbrough it was called Regional Football. We'd play York, and all the local clubs who had all signed pre-War pros that happened to be in the area. As they came and went they'd apply for games here and there. You had a professional game almost every week."

So you signed for Boro as a Wartime player?

"I signed in May 1943, the Sports Officer at Marske said Boro wanted me to play for them. They'd been scouting I think. After I'd played, Wilf Gillow, the manager, called me in and asked me to sign pro. He offered me £1 10 shillings a match, which was quite a lot more than the Army paid. So I said 'where do I sign?' But I didn't realise how tight the contracts were - it was slavery. There was no way you could get away from the club unless they wanted you to go. When I came back from Burma, I was posted to Barnard Castle for the few months before demob. As I was under contract, Boro started playing me. I told the manager, David Jack, that I was going back to London after demob, to try and find a club - I didn't tell him I'd been fishing for a club already. He said, 'if you want to play football, you've got to come back here. I'm not going to let you go.' Play at Boro, or not at all. That was the power they had. Fortunately there were quite a few games in London, so it wasn't too bad."

Wilf Gillow was the Boro manager pre-War and built a highly rated team. What did you think of him?

"He was a gentleman, he was a father figure and was getting on a bit. I think I was one of the last pros he signed. David Jack, who succeeded Gillow, was one of my heroes. I watched him play for the Arsenal as a kid. Dad and I went to Arsenal one week and Chelsea the next.

I played against him funnily enough. After he retired he worked for Barclays Bank and played for them. Before I came to Middlesbrough, I played for Dulwich Hamlet and we played all the big banks because they owned huge sports grounds. He didn't remember me kicking him up the backside - maybe because he liked a drink he'd forgotten the incident! But he was a wonderful player at Middlesbrough and was part of a good footballing side."

Why didn't Boro make the breakthrough and win something?

"There wasn't that killer instinct somehow. We always played good football; there were a lot of internationals at the club. George Camsell and Micky Fenton were there, then after that, you had Clough and Peacock."

Camsell and Fenton were both given jobs at the club when they retired, how did younger players like yourself relate to people like that?

"When you were a young pro, you stood to attention, 'yes sir, no sir, three bags full sir'. You didn't butt in. It wasn't until you were a senior player you were taken seriously. But when I became a senior player the youngsters would then tell you to 'eff-off. That was how it had evolved."

How good was the best Boro team you played in?

"It's difficult to say, Boro were a good First Division side. At that time you were playing against the best players and clubs in the world - Stan Matthews, Tom Finney, Portsmouth, Manchester United and Newcastle - they were all great sides. Although the football was slower, I think it was more skillful."

How tactical was the game after the War?

"Football is only difficult when it's fancy. I went with the Football League side to Ireland to play the Irish League. It used to be like an England B side. The Football League team would play a Scottish League team and the Irish League. Walter Winterbottom was the English coach. I was a reserve for the team, so I was sat at the back with Eddie Bailey from Tottenham. Walter was talking about zone defence and man for man marking; 'we'll do this and we won't do that'. I said to Eddie, 'What are the Irish boys doing when we're doing all this?' He said, 'Don't take any notice of him, we let him go on and then we go out and play football.'

You can plan set pieces, but once that ball starts rolling, I don't know what you're going to do; you don't know what I'm going to do. That's where the skill comes in. The trouble was, if you didn't listen to these chaps, you never got picked. There were very few people who could tell the manager where to go and still get picked - Wilf Mannion was one. You could argue with the manager, but you had to be a little bit careful or you wouldn't play the next week. I'd just got myself recognised. I'd been picked to play for England B but I wasn't told about it. I was in Middlesbrough with my wife when she spotted it on a newspaper placard outside the Town Hall.

I'd got these minor honours playing full-back but the manager, Bob Dennison, told me I'd never make it in that position, even after being picked to play for England there. I think that's what stopped me progressing, because I played every position on the park. You find the same thing now, managers have their favourites, players who play to their system."

What sort of a player were you?

"I was fast, two footed, good in the air, good in the tackle. I was on the team sheet in nine positions, and I played in goal in the F.A Cup against Leicester after our 'keeper Ugolini got injured. Wilf was captain and Johnny Spuhler was the recognised deputy goalkeeper, but he didn't want to go in. Wilf went round the whole lot, none of them would go in. 'You can't say no, get the bloody shirt on,' he said to me. We drew nil-nil but lost the replay at Filbert Street."

What was Mannion like to play with?

"He was a great player, but it was instinctive. He wasn't a schemer. He did things with the ball, like Gazza, but you never knew where to go for him. You'd go wide and deep for him and he'd go on your blind side.

The next time you'd think, bugger it I'll stay, and he'd knock it long down the line - it was very difficult. But as a manipulator of the ball he was great, you can't dispute that. But sometimes these geniuses are difficult to handle."

Was he one of the lads in the dressing room?

"There was very little fraternisation, you'd be surprised. You'd get in half an hour before a game and have a chin wag, but once the game was finished you went off. There weren't clubs or places like that to go to.

The whole time I was at Middlesbrough my wife had to wait outside for me after the game. If it was tanking down, she still had to wait outside. All the directors would go past, say 'hello', but never think of letting her in. They were the businessmen - the players were just hired hands."

It's probably the same now, there's a lot of people getting into football and making a lot of money.

"They're not sports people. One of the Middlesbrough directors was on the board of England selectors, but when he went in to the dressing room he had to have the programme in his hand. Even if he was talking to you he wouldn't know your name until he'd had a look at the back of your shirt.

It was funny if late changes were made before a game. But he stopped me once on Linthorpe Road. There was a World Cup coming up, he asked if I wanted to go. Not to play, just to travel with the squad. Having just got married, I said no. But that was the kind of power they had."

Did you enjoy playing North East derbies?

"We always enjoyed playing Newcastle. Sunderland were vicious. [Laughs] I hated the sight of Sunderland. They were kicking each other before the game, that was the attitude. But we had some great games with Newcastle. It was Newcastle that drew the record attendance to Ayresome Park, fifty-three thousand."

That must have been a great time to be watching football.

"Arsenal had nine or ten internationals. Alex James was a magician, he would direct his winger, Cliff Bastin, where to go. That was a supreme side in England. They did what pros should do, they delivered every week. You see an awful lot of players now who don't seem to be giving ninety minutes. You can't always produce ninety minutes of quality, but you should always be running and creating a nuisance."

Boro fans, in my time, have never tolerated lazy players. Was it the same when you played?

"If you can't run for ninety minutes, you should pack it up. Maybe players now have so much money they don't really care. It must affect them."

Motivation must be a problem if you're twenty-nine and already a multi-millionnaire?

"Then they start looking for a few transfers! Some players are taking their clubs to the cleaners."

As Ravanelli did to us.

"I was glad when he went, his Cup Final display was daylight robbery - he only went on the field for the medal."

A lot of less gifted players contributed a lot more to the club.

"I can't think of a reason why eleven men all playing their guts out in a team should be paid differently. I didn't like it when Jimmy Hill, who was the PFA leader, abolished the maximum wage and I don't like it now."

If you had the power would you impose a wage ceiling?

"I would have a standard contract. If the team is good all the players get paid according to what they win. There are a lot of clubs now in debt, they're not earning their keep. When my brother Alan was manager at Bristol City he took them into the old First Division.

The Directors told him to get all the best players tied down on contracts but Alan told them he wasn't comfortable with that. He did it, but before their contracts were up, City got relegated and nearly went bust. Clubs are still doing it today so they don't lose players due to Bosman."

Was the maximum wage a fair wage?

"I think so. When it was abolished the maximum wage was about £24, plus £4 for a win - but that doesn't sound very much today."

It doesn't sound a lot if your career is over at thirty-five.

"When Jimmy Hill fought his case for the maximum wage to be abolished, it was so that Johnny Haynes could get his £100 a week. The season following abolition, a third of all professional footballers were sacked just so that clubs could pay their stars more money. Before that, clubs would have about thirty-five pros but once clubs started paying the big boys, a lot of players weren't offered contracts."

When they were getting 30 or 40,000 people into Ayresome Park it makes you wonder what happened to all the money?

"I don't know where the money went, I suppose they might not have been taking that much?"

After being in the top flight since 1929 Boro were relegated in 1954. How hard did it hit you?

" I thought it was the end of the world, but you never think it's going to happen, you always think you'll get two points next week and everything will work out fine."

1948 – Ronnie Dicks beats Chelsea's Ken Armstrong to shoot during a 1-0 away defeat

Why do you think it happened?

"We didn't score enough goals. Scoring goals is the biggest mystery in the game."

Talking about scoring goals, how do you rate Brian Clough?

"He was good in as much as he was a prolific goalscorer. His attitude was that he was there to score goals, and he did. I never argued with him. But when he wasn't scoring, he wasn't interested. He wouldn't try to open the game up and get Alan Peacock in. When Walter Winterbottom picked him for England he told Brian to go wide. He asked me what he should do as I was captain at the time. I didn't get on with him. I told him he had no choice. He was never given a run in the England side."

How good was George Hardwick?

"Classical. He was a ball playing full-back. He wasn't very quick, but he had a strong tackle, two good feet and he could pass the ball. That's everything you need in a full-back - he was very much like Alf Ramsey. Ramsey couldn't sprint either, whereas most defenders now are like lightning.

It was due to an injury to George that I played left-back - we were at Blackpool and George had to go off, meaning I switched from outside-right. Being two-footed it didn't bother me but I didn't realise for some time that the Blackpool outside-right that day was Stan Matthews!"

You must have played against all the great players of your era?

"Tom Finney, Nat Lofthouse, Len Shackleton - all the great players."

A lot of people now see the post-War years as a golden age of football. Did you think of it like that at the time?

"No, it was just Saturday to Saturday to Saturday. There wasn't the furore about football then. There was no European Cup, there was just club football and the fact that the working man had nothing else on Saturday. Television wasn't rampant, that was why you regularly got 40,000 at Ayresome Park."

What was it like to play in front of 40,000 at Ayresome Park?

"It was great and the reserves used to get 10 to 12,000 too."

What was the atmosphere like?

"You got used to it. The only time it was nasty was if you were playing badly, then they started to get at you. At Ayresome Park you were some distance from the crowd, but when we went away Lindy Delaphena got some stick at times."

Was that because he was one of the first black players in English football?

"Yes, it was because he was black. He was a nice lad, well educated"

Was there a section of the crowd who would single a player out for stick?

"No. Occasionally we'd have a player who shouldn't really have been playing. We had a player called Martin Reagan who was very fast, practically ten seconds for the hundred yards, but he would run the ball out too often. He used to say to the crowd, 'I don't know what you're complaining about, I give you enough of the ball.'

A lot of them didn't appreciate it but I can't really think of anyone else who got any badmouthing. But when we went into town, it was a pleasure, people would stop you, the only trouble was they wanted to talk. I was a complete stranger, but if you played for them and did your best, they took you to their hearts. Which is the way it should be."

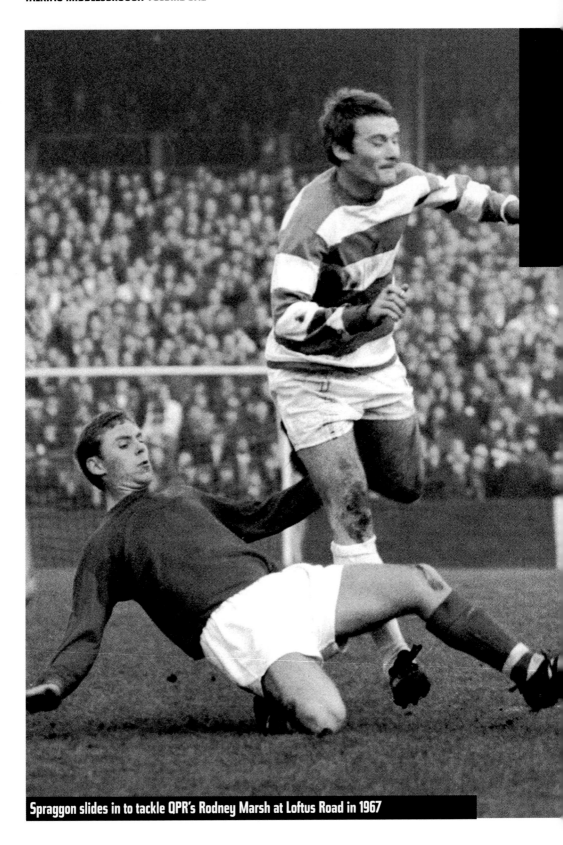

Spraggon slides in to tackle QPR's Rodney Marsh at Loftus Road in 1967

Frank Spraggon

Frank Spraggon was a one club man, apart from one game for Hartlepool, and a spell playing in America. A Newcastle fan as a boy, he made his Boro debut as a seventeen-year-old and played in the five-three defeat at Cardiff in 1966 which sent the club to the old Third Division for the first time. He was a regular after Boro were promoted back to the Second Division and played in a variety of positions as the team always fell short of promotion between 1968 and 1973. Jack Charlton made him first choice left back for the all conquering 1973-74 season and he played most of the following season in the First Division. Terry Cooper was brought in around transfer deadline time to replace him in 1974-1975. By now in the veteran stage of his career, he played in America before retiring due to a knee problem. I remembered Frank Spraggon very much as a team player. Happy to do his own job, while other players grabbed the headlines. This impression was reinforced when we met. He was quick to pass on credit for his success to others, whilst acknowledging his own shortcomings. He now works as a coach at the Middlesbrough Academy in Eston.

Did you always know that you'd be a footballer?

"Yes, full stop. I left school in 1960, and coming from a mining village, it was either football or go down the pits. There weren't many people on the dole then. I was always into sport but football was my first love. I had the choice of a few clubs, but coming from the Newcastle area, I was so disappointed when the only club that didn't come in for me was Newcastle.

There were a few clubs in for me including West Brom, but I decided to go to Preston. Would you believe I was homesick at Deepdale? It's only down the road! Then Middlesbrough got in touch, and apart from leaving as a player, I've remained there all my life.

I knew I wanted to stay in the game after retiring too so I got my qualifications early, which has stood me in good stead. I've been all over the world coaching, Sweden, Holland and America."

Was it strange being a Newcastle fan playing for Boro in derbies?

"Yes. We used to play back-to-back games over Christmas and Easter, Middlesbrough played Newcastle at Ayresome Park one day and the return was at St James' the next.

Bryan Orritt, [Welsh utility player from 1962-1966] got injured in the home game and as I played in his position, I knew I'd be playing the next day at Newcastle. To go up there and play was a dream come true, there were fifty thousand people there and I vividly remember that the pitch was rock hard and rutted.

I think we got beat 2-1, but it was my first derby match at the age of nineteen. Coming from Newcastle, Sunderland were always the real enemy, I used to love those games. Playing against little Bobby Kerr, he came through the juniors at Sunderland while I was coming through at Ayresome Park - we had some good clashes. But when I first went to Middlesbrough I played for the first team before I played for the reserves, which is unique. I was seventeen, having played for the two junior teams I was called up by Raich Carter for a League Cup game against Bradford Park Avenue. But after that I went in the reserves."

There were a few local lads in the team when you started, was that a deliberate policy because there was no money, or was there just a lot of local talent around at the time?

"Middlesbrough always had a good youth policy. They always had good young players coming through and there was a really good set up behind the scenes. My father-in-law, Harold Shepherdson, was in charge at one point and he had a good network across in Ireland and Scotland; he had great connections especially in the North East. He found some good kids from the Newcastle area and a few made the grade."

Of the apprentices that were with you, how many made it?

"Let me think, a lad called Don Heath, who played for Swindon when they won the League Cup in 1969, and Arthur Horsfield a centre-forward who left Boro for Newcastle are the two obvious ones. There was also a lad called Cliffy Wright, who only played a couple of times for Middlesbrough, but played a lot of games for Hartlepool."

Harold Shepherdson was England number two as well as being Boro's assistant manager - did it help when you married his daughter?

"Yes and no!" [laughs]

You must have got slaughtered for it?

"A lot of people said it was to get my game, but it made it harder I thought. But when it came to tickets there were no problems. [Laughs] Cup Final tickets, World Cup tickets, it had its perks. I must admit Harold helped me in a lot of ways, not just in football. He helped and supported us in our marriage too. But there was many a time he gave me a rollocking, [laughs] which I suppose was only for my own good.

He used to tell me the things I was doing wrong which were many, and point me in the right direction. He was very supportive because football was his life as well. Fifty-plus years at Middlesbrough, England trainer, four World Cup tournaments, you can't get much better than that can you?"

Do you think he's got the recognition he deserves for everything he did at Boro?

"I'll have to be careful what I say here. Under the current Boro chairman, yes."

Who was your room-mate at Boro?

"John Hickton, we always used to room together. Willie Maddren and Graeme Souness were good pals too, Graeme was single and used to chase the women back then. He came round for his tea a lot and we still keep in contact although he's a millionaire now. [Laughs] But John and I always shared a room. Why they put us together I don't know.

Craggsy and Millsy roomed together, so did Foggon and Murdoch - now there's a combination! We never used to venture into their room. I haven't seen John since he left. Unfortunately when they had the reunion at the last game at Ayresome Park, I was in France, so I missed it all."

Was it fun to play in the promotion team in 1974, or would Jack go mad at players if they put a foot wrong?

"A lot of people have said to me that if Jack Charlton's defence had been playing at Wembley in 1978, we wouldn't have conceded that late equaliser. We would have shut up shop. I know it's easy to say, but we would have put the ball into the stands, which is where it needed to be, because all Boro needed was a result. We knew if we went one up, there weren't many teams that would score against us. Two up and the game was won. We played to our strengths.

Jack did rollock us a couple of times though. We had Newcastle at home one game where we were winning 3-1; game over. But they scored twice in the final seconds. He went through Platty like a dose of salts. At full time Jack was waiting in the tunnel with the tea urn - as we came off he threw it at Platty. [Laughs] We used to joke that he dropped it. But Jack was okay."

Did it bother you that the press called that team boring?
"No. It made us more determined. We went to Fulham one night and put four past them, went to West Brom and got another four. But we knew the result was the most important thing."

In the last home game of the 1973-1974 season, having already won the Division Two Championship, Boro beat Sheffield Wednesday 8-0.
"When we went to Hillsborough for the Cup Final Replay, a car park attendant said 'I recognise you, don't I? You're a Middlesbrough lad.' I said 'You might have seen me when we put eight past you.' Thinking about it now, there were some good players in that Wednesday side. That game was unbelievable."

Is that season the highlight of your career?
"Without a doubt. We knew we were promoted by Easter. Jack always used to tell us early on, settle for a point because at the end of the season they all add up. But if we'd known we were going to be twenty points clear at the end we needn't have bothered. He got us organised at free kicks and throw ins, cross-over throw ins, short free kicks - we got away with murder but we knew what we were doing."

In Jack Charlton's autobiography he tells a story about you not being the best passer in the world. Is that fair?
"Yes, I'd go along with that, I was good at defending but David Armstrong used to do my work for me. In his book he says I had a knock on the head which affected my vision, which is not quite true. I had an operation on my knee and when I came round I found I couldn't see out of one eye. That was my excuse for a bad game [Laughs]. So I had to adjust. But I didn't feel sorry for myself, not when you see people with serious injuries

and illnesses - like my friend Willie Maddren. There's nothing wrong with me. But passing wasn't one of my strengths although I must have added something because he kept me in the side."

A lot of players from the 60's and 70's say it was a much harder game then. Who was the hardest man physically you played against?

"We played at Coventry one night. They had a centre-half called George Curtis, who was manager with Sillett when they won the FA Cup in 1987. God he was hard. With sleeves rolled up in the middle of winter, he used to come up for corners and clear everyone out of his way.

People talk about Norman Hunter and Tommy Smith being hard-men but I thought they could play and were fair, not really fierce... I used to keep out of George Curtis' way though!"

You were more or less a one-club man. If you could have your career again would you look to move around a bit more?

"Yes and no. Obviously the money then was nothing like what players earn now but as I married a local girl I wasn't keen on moving any how. I had a good career and I was happy at Middlesbrough. Having said that, if a top club comes in for you..."

Near the end of your career you played in America. How did that arise?

"Jack had told me I was going to be released at the end of the season and that he knew English managers in America who were looking for players. One of them was Freddy Goodwin, a Busby Babe who went on to manage Birmingham. He was starting a team in Minnesota so I took the opportunity to go for six months.

Although I was struggling with my bad knee, I really enjoyed it. I played against Pele, and had my picture taken with him, which was one of the highlights of my career. Eusebio, George Best and Bobby Moore were there. Beckenbauer went after I left, along with the Dutch legend Neeskens.

I travelled all over America and had a great time, during a period when the league was a great success. It died a death later, because in America you've got to win, you have to win. Losing is no good. Attendances went down, and as they say in America, they want bums on seats because the owners put a lot of money in. Then they started the indoor league up, now they've got the outdoor league again, which looks like taking off.

But it's different coaching in America to Europe. Kids are brought up with baseball and American football - give me an English kid any time, especially one from Grangetown or South Bank; they're just naturals."

How did you come to work for Middlesbrough as a coach?

"I was involved with the school of excellence, with Ron Bone, who was the youth development officer. Then the club started an academy similar to the Football In The Community scheme. It's called The Middlesbrough Academy and involves going round schools offering coaching and things like that.

It's going to get established and take off and will provide a way of helping kids in the area - you never know if there's any budding Juninhos. I can name four or five kids now who really impress and who have a chance. This is what you have to do. You have to catch them at grass roots. If you have one who goes on to be worth millions it has to be worthwhile."

Especially in an area like ours which produces so many footballers.

"I can't believe it. People say there's not many good youngsters around, but there are. Kids just need a little bit of help."

What was the worst result while you were playing for Boro?

"We went to Nottingham Forest and got turned over by five in our promotion year, I remember Duncan McKenzie ran me ragged; he ran all of us ragged. I also remember going to QPR when Stan Anderson was manager - I couldn't get near Rodney Marsh that day. Then there was a winger who played for Leicester called Keith Weller. He was a flying machine. But I think getting turned over at Nottingham Forest was the worst feeling."

Didn't you play in the FA Cup Quarter-Final against Birmingham as well?

"Yes, we'd beaten them twice in the League but we just didn't perform that day. It was so disappointing. Looking back to that game, and going to Wembley and Hillsborough during the 1996-1997 season as a spectator, I really feel for the supporters. At Birmingham we let them down badly. It was heartbreaking."

People have said that Jack Charlton was to blame for the Quarter-Final defeat because he only wanted a draw, then a replay at Ayresome Park. Is there any truth in that?

"Yes and no. Alan Foggon didn't perform that day, I think they man marked him well, like Leicester did with Juninho in the League Cup Final. Most of the time Alan could murder defences, but he didn't perform; as a team we didn't perform. It was a big, big disappointment, because we were expected to beat City. To make the defeat worse the other teams left in the Cup were sides like Fulham, who got beaten by West Ham in the Final. Teams we could turn over. It was a nightmare."

If Stan Anderson had stayed on as manager for a couple more seasons would he have got promotion?

"It's hard to say... I don't think so, Charlton brought Bobby Murdoch in and he got Souness to really start playing. I think Stan had taken us as far as he could. His ideas weren't rubbing off any more and I think it needed a fresh face. Jack certainly sorted us out when he arrived."

What did he say to you?

"He said we had some good players, some bad players, and some average players. We all wondered which category we were in. But he got us organised and made us play to our strengths. He bought Bobby Murdoch in, who was a great passer of a ball, and took it from there."

Do you think that Charlton's team should have gone on to win something in the top flight?

"Well, it was there for the taking and a lot of people say that he should have splashed out on a goal-scorer. But knowing Jack he didn't like spending money, something I think he now regrets. We could have also done with a bit more luck at times too."

What would you say was the best game you ever played?

"[Laughs] That's a hard one... I remember going to Coventry one night and although it was only a 0-0 draw we all played very well. Even Jack said 'well done' to me! I remember going to Sunderland and beating them by four goals too, I played well that day. But what I remember more is getting good results here and there and helping the team in my own little way."

Peter Creamer

Peter Creamer was unfortunate to be a defender at Boro from 1970-75, when the club was particularly strong in that department. Primarily a right-back, he was reserve to John Craggs, arguably the best man ever to play for Boro in that position. He made his debut in the 1972-73 season and played six games. He made a further three appearances in the promotion season of 1973-74. His first team opportunities were limited, and after a fall out with Jack Charlton he asked to be put on the transfer list. He moved to York and played out his career in the lower divisions and non-League football. As Peter Creamer was a name I remembered from my early days watching Boro, it was interesting to discover what had happened to him. He had more than his share of bad luck in the game, but when we talked in the pub he ran in Middlesbrough, he was happy to share the stories of good times and bad.

You could have signed for Manchester United as a schoolboy. Who persuaded you to sign for Boro?

"It was Harold Shepherdson and Stan Anderson. David Mills and I followed the same pattern; if he hadn't signed for Middlesbrough, he would have signed for Manchester United too. United offered both of us apprenticeships, whereas Middlesbrough said they would sign me as a pro at seventeen. At United it was 'get to eighteen and we'll see', so I didn't take much persuasion. You knew Stan would give you your chance if you were good enough. That was maybe Stan's downfall, because when Jack Charlton came he never changed the pattern of play. He would keep the same team, whereas Stan might make three or four changes.

If you look at the North East, Middlesbrough are probably still the best for bringing young lads through; Harold Shepherdson and Ray Grant did just that. Harold Shepherdson was Alf Ramsey's number two for the England team, so you can imagine what it was like when he knocked on my door."

How would you describe yourself as a player?

"I played full back for the first team but I was centre-half throughout my schooldays. But I played for England schoolboys as a full-back. It was ironic because I made my debut for England against the Republic of Ireland, and my mam came from the Republic. This was before Jack exploited the rule changes and brought a lot of English born lads in. As a player I suppose I was good enough as a First Division reserve player, but given the chance in the first team I never let myself or the team down. I was always on the fringe but never proven really."

What was the longest run you got in the side?

"It was three games over Christmas, because John Craggs always fancied time off at Christmas. I would get in if he was suspended or injured, but he was never injured long enough! Jack's policy was that if the full-back's injured, the reserve full back comes in. Not like Stan Anderson who would make two or three positional changes. Jack made one. If Craggsy got injured I was in. I just wish he'd got injured more often. A broken leg or something, sorry Craggsy!

I'm not saying this because I was his understudy, but I think John Craggs should have got an England cap. When Steve Whitworth got selected ahead of him I thought it was an injustice, because he wasn't in the same class as Craggsy. Then we had Terry Cooper on the other side. Frank Spraggon always did a great job, but if you had to pick Terry Cooper or Frank Spraggon I think Frank would admit you'd choose 'T.C.' Then when you've got Stuart Boam and Willie Maddren. There's no way anyone else was going to play in place of them. I was good enough to replace anyone in the back four temporarily, but not good enough to shift them."

Is it true to say you've had your share of bad luck?

"It was funny, we were playing Manchester City at home once and I was in the squad. We'd gone to the Marton Country Club, as we always did, and Jack had announced the team. I wasn't in it so I asked Jack if I could go home, get changed and go to the match. He agreed. So I met my father-in-law, had a couple of pints, and went to the ground.

When we got there I had a pasty and a Bovril. Then the tannoy announcer said, "Peter Creamer, please report to the dressing room, immediately!" When I got there I found out that Craggsy had been talking to Dennis Tueart in the tunnel and had fainted. I had to get ready. I went straight to the toilet, stuck my fingers down my throat and got rid of the beer, pasty and Bovril. While I was doing that Craggsy was on the smelling salts. Not only did he recover, he was well enough to play. Jack said, 'unlucky again, Peter.' Not only wasn't I playing, but I was starving! So yes, I was unlucky [laughs].

Another time, we went down to Ipswich. Craggsy had his ankle in plaster, so I thought I was definitely playing. I got a good night's sleep in the hotel, I felt really good. We went for some light training the morning of the game and there's Craggsy with the plaster off. I couldn't believe it, he needed a walking stick on the bus down. When Jack asked how it was, he said it was good, so Craggsy's played. Then, about ten minutes into the game, he shouted to the bench to say that his ankle had gone again. Jack told him he'd have to stay on as I wasn't even on the bench!"

Did you fall out with Jack about not getting a game?

"Yes I did. I always wanted to play. We were playing Aston Villa at home one week and I got a note through the door which said to report to the ground at twelve o'clock. I got there about fifteen minutes early to find Jack had already picked the team and Frank Spraggon was playing. Why send for me if the decision had already been made? Jack said he didn't know if I'd turn up. I told him I lived for playing. On the following Tuesday I asked for a transfer."

And that was how you came to leave Boro?

"Yes, I'd just come back from the States, where I'd been playing for Dallas in the summer season. I asked Harold Shepherdson and Jack if I could play abroad, because there was a lack of opportunities in the first team. They said get yourself fixed up. The first team were going on a World tour, but I couldn't afford to go on £50 basic per week in the reserves, especially with a wife and small child. The other lads were single, but that was my choice. The offer came and I went. I played against Pele twice, so that's my claim to fame. I went from £50 per week to £250, and had the chance to stay longer but decided to come back. Again there were limited first team opportunities, although I played against Manchester United in the League Cup Quarter Final, we drew nil-nil, but got beat three-nil in the replay, which I didn't play in. But the Villa team selection trick was a sickener to be honest, so I asked to go on the transfer list.

The finances were a factor as well. For playing the one game against Manchester United, I earned over £600. If the basic had been better than £50 it would have been more encouraging to stay on. I was twenty-two, but I'd been at Middlesbrough for eight years, and I wasn't going to oust Craggsy or Terry Cooper; we had a brilliant back four. The other thing was our reserve League wasn't strong enough. You'd play Sunderland one week, then it would be Notts County or Grimsby. We needed to be in the Central League playing against Liverpool and Manchester United. To test the players you need to be playing against quality."

Was it just the one season in America?
"Yes, we could have gone back, but I'd moved by then. I went to York City on loan because Wilf McGuinness was there. He'd looked after the schoolboys when I'd been at Manchester United. Derrick Downing and Eric McMordie were also at York then, as was John Stone, who'd played a couple of games for Boro. While I was at City Stan Anderson made an offer for Brian Taylor and myself, and we both went to Doncaster in a £30,000 deal, which was good."

How long were you there for?
"I stayed there ten months, then I went to Hartlepool. After one defeat Stan put the whole team up for sale. The following Tuesday I signed for Hartlepool and stayed there two years."

What were Hartlepool like at the time?
"Not a very good side, I've got to be honest. It was made up of older pros on their last club, younger pros coming through, and people like myself who were trying to reconstruct a career. Hartlepool wasn't a good club. It's a fabulous club now, but in those days, very poor. It was first team football though. Whereas with Stan, at Middlesbrough and Doncaster, he would chop and change. I played eight positions in ten months for Stan, you would give your best, but you prefer to be settled. I was happy to come to Hartlepool."

What happened after you left Hartlepool?
"After my second season at Hartlepool we had to apply for re-election. The whole club needed restructuring. I was one of the first players to

get freedom of contract. The career wasn't going the way I wanted it to. I realised early on that I wouldn't be going to Liverpool or West Ham. So you think, 'where would I like to play?' But I realised that clubs that were doing well weren't going to come in for me. It would be clubs looking for someone to do a job. Having a family to bring up, I realised football wasn't the be all and end all and started to think about settling down after all the moves. After Hartlepool I went to Millwall for three months.

Nothing happened there. I wasn't that disappointed because London wasn't the place for me so I found a job in a steelworks earning much better money than I was on at Hartlepool. Then Peter Madden, who had been manager of Darlington, took over at Rochdale and asked me to go there with him.

I was a free agent so I played the rest of that season and we avoided re-election. Bobby Scaife was there, another ex-Boro lad, and I thought it was great. I was swapping shifts at the steelworks to play for Rochdale, then out of the blue I got a phone call asking if we would consider going to Australia. The guy who was ringing us was in his shorts in ninety degrees of heat and here it was snowing and we'd just been thrashed at Huddersfield - I didn't take much persuading. While we were in Australia, Peter Brine and Tony Dickinson, two old Boro lads were in Tasmania. There are old Boro players everywhere!

When I got home I started playing for Gateshead in the Northern Premier League at the same time as working for a courier company. After that we sold the house and bought a pub in Bishop Auckland. As well as running the pub I also did some work with a guy called Dave Richardson who was a P.E. teacher from Middlesbrough. He went on to work on youth development for Aston Villa and Leicester but we were working for the Premier League, looking after lads who had signed schoolboy forms for Premiership clubs outside the north east. They came to us one night a week for training, so that when they went to their clubs, they weren't behind the lads who lived locally."

Do you think there is still the talent at grassroots in the North East?

"Boro have quite a few coming through now, but when I was there, we had lads like, Malcolm Smith, Pat Cuff and Billy Woof - we were all ready to play because we trained with and against the senior players. You lived for playing and dreamt of it all the time. It's interesting that the youngsters who have come in for Boro recently have all done well.

But if you look at the North East as a whole in the past few years, Middlesbrough have brought on about five or six young players, Sunderland maybe three or four... Newcastle none."

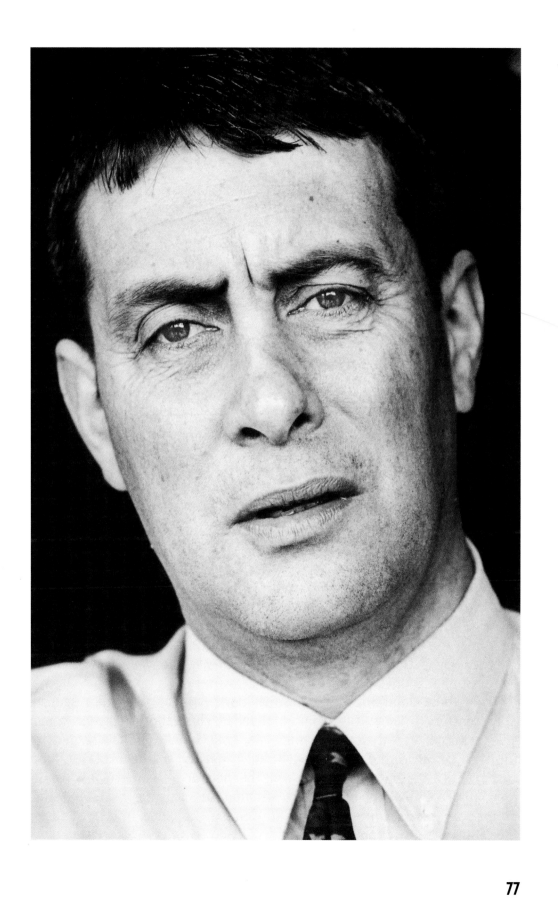

Wasn't your son also with Boro for a while?

"Yes, he followed in my footsteps. He was at Aston Villa as a schoolboy and signed as an apprentice for Boro. But I don't think he was treated well by George Shipley and Lennie Lawrence. David Mills's son was there at the time and he was also treated badly in my opinion."

What was the problem?

"I don't know, I believed he was worth a chance and he wasn't given one. After he left Boro he had a week at Blackpool with Billy Ayre, who's a friend of mine. He scored goals, Billy liked him, and said he could do something for the following season. Billy got sacked the next day [laughs]. My other son's more academic, but from the age of twelve Christopher knew what he was going to do. And he nearly made it."

Did you enjoy playing for Gateshead?

"Yes. We had some good players, all ex-pros like Kenny Ellis, who's since died sadly, Stevie Holbrook, Les Mutrie. We could knock it around and mix it, if necessary. You had to try to keep out of bother as well because you didn't want to have to take time off work. I had a few knocks and stitches when I was a pro, but the minute I stopped playing pro I left my nose on a lads elbow at Northallerton.

We kicked off at three and I was in the Infirmary at five past. My face was covered in blood, it was coming out of my mouth. What a mess. The doctor walked in and asked what I'd done. Joking, I told him it was my ankle. He said, 'let's get your boot off then!' [Laughs] I ended up having plastic surgery."

Do you object to Boro's big name signings and the wages they get paid?

"No, I think it's a sign of the times. I remember my dad talking about great players, but I thought 'that's in the past, let's think about the present'. Now I think players were better twenty-odd years ago! People like McMordie, Souness, Murdoch.

What would John Hickton be worth now? Twenty-plus goals season after season. I know the game's changed, but those players could have adapted. It's a hundred miles an hour now. You now expect a full-back to have the same touch as a quality midfield player, not someone like myself who would win the ball and then maybe give it away again. Defenders now aren't winning the ball as much and the referee's interpretation of the laws are ruining the game. You need tackling; a bit of physical presence."

You can't have football without tackling can you?

"And kicking people from behind, biting and punching them [laughs]. It was a more physical game. Arsenal always had a physical presence, so you had to match them. Not to the extent of Leeds against Chelsea say, where it was a bloodbath, but the tackles did fly in. Some naughty lads were play-ing in those days. Little John Giles and Eric McMordie; they wouldn't think twice about putting you in hospital. But they were good players."

Who was the best player you played with at Boro?

"There were a few, but I'd have to say McMordie. Souness was coming through, Murdoch was a fabulous player but he was coming towards the end. Boam and Maddren weren't internationals. I played with McMordie at York and Hartlepool as well as Boro. He had two good feet, always showed, put his foot in, great enthusiasm. He had to win, he gave plenty of praise, plenty of criticism, but always constructive. He was small in stature, but he was big on the field."

Gary Gill

Gary Gill in aerial action during a night match at Ayresome Park in 1986

Gary Gill was one of a crop of young local players who took the club to two successive promotions in the late 80's. Following liquidation in 1986, manager Bruce Rioch was left with no choice but to field a young, largely home-grown team. Gary Gill was part of the group which included Tony Mowbray, Gary Parkinson, Gary Pallister, Colin Cooper and Stuart Ripley. In 1986-87 Gary Gill played thirty-three games as Boro were promoted to the Second Division. He was replaced by Dean Glover as Boro were promoted to the First Division via the play-offs in 1988. After a long wait in the reserves, he was given a chance in March 1989, and was in the form of his life until breaking a leg in April 1989. Despite making a full recovery he had a series of disagreements with Bruce Rioch which led to his leaving the club to join then non-League Darlington. He refound his form under former Boro coach Brian Little, and was part of the Darlington team which was promoted to the Third Division. After retiring through injury he worked as a summariser for BBC Radio Cleveland, and as joint-manager at Gateshead in the Northern League.

How did you first make your name as a player?

"As a schoolboy, Middlesbrough had a very good town team. We were the first schoolboy team from Middlesbrough to win a national trophy, so from there we all got picked up by professional clubs, even the squad players. Very few actually made it but that was how Middlesbrough originally noticed me."

Were any other clubs chasing you?

"Yeah, I could have gone to a few places, but wasn't interested. In my first year at Senior School, Manchester City contacted me; one of the teachers was a scout for them. I said thanks but I'd wait until Middlesbrough came in for me. All the lads were the same. Now you get parents trying to screw clubs for money but money wasn't an issue then."

You were obviously a Boro fan, who were your heroes at the time?

"I used to like David Hodgson, which is ironic because I ended up as his boot boy and I got to play with him. He'll be a good manager, I'm convinced. He talks very well, his teams play football the right way, and he knows the game."

You could argue that he never fulfilled his potential as a player, and maybe that will help him succeed as a manager, as it did Brian Clough.

"He could have been better as a player I suppose, who couldn't? The problem was he didn't score enough goals. He was a great player, but he might get six, seven, or eight goals a season. As a striker you've got to be in double figures."

Who signed you for Boro?

"Bobby Murdoch signed me as an apprentice but Malcolm Allison gave me my debut as a sub."

Did you realise what state the club was in when you signed?

"When I signed the club was okay and seemed in a sound position. I didn't care anyway, I was only a young lad. The club's finances were the last thing on my mind. I just had to clean David Hodgson's boots, among others. As long as I did that, and played a bit of football, that was all that mattered. At that time things went well for me, I got in the first team at eighteen. It was a struggling side it has to be said. Malcolm Allison was in charge and he wanted to get rid of a lot of the older boys who were earning a lot more money. He gave debuts to people like Alan Roberts, he chucked us all in, and I got a few games towards the end of the season when Big Jack took temporary charge. Willie had taken over by the start of the following season and he gave me an extended run in the side which created interest from people inside and outside the club. Unfortunately I slipped two discs in my back just after my nineteenth birthday so that put my progress back for a while. After that it was injury after injury for a spell. The club itself was struggling through relegation, but this was prior to liquidation in 1986 when it really started to get a bit naughty."

What was it like playing in front of 4,000 crowds at Ayresome Park?

"To quote Willie Maddren, 'they were sparse and hostile.'

It was difficult because they were diehards; that was all that were left, but a lot of them were cynical. A lot seemed to actually enjoy us failing. It gave them a great excuse to call us what they liked. The worst thing about that was, because they were small crowds, you could hear every single comment and put faces to the phrases. But at the time I was play-ing okay. We all got stick because we were bottom of the league. It was a difficult time for everyone, but the camaraderie between the lads never dipped which was good."

When the club did go into liquidation, why did you choose to stay?

"At the time we'd just been relegated to the Third Division, but all of us could have got other clubs. It was a rule that if you hadn't been paid for six weeks you were entitled to a free transfer, I believe that's how Peter Beagrie left. But I don't hold that against him, I never will. Brian Laws tried to leave the same way. I think looking at the game now, players care much more about money then they did then. People blamed players for trying to leave the club, but if you haven't been paid for six weeks and there's a strong possibility that the club will finish, what are you supposed to do?"

The older players must have been family men as well.

"That's right. I was single, as most of us were at the time, so I just hung on. I thought, 'If the club survives, something good could come out of this', which is exactly what happened."

Kicking off that season at Hartlepool, did you have any idea what would happen in the next couple of years?

"You could sense something. There was a bare squad of just fifteen play-ers. We knew we were struggling and not even playing at our own ground. We drew that first game. I remember Archie Stephens getting two of the best goals he ever scored. Particularly the second one, the volley, which was ridiculous for Archie, who doesn't score goals like that. But you could sense something was going to happen. The next few outings we were winning games that we shouldn't have won. We were playing well and winning games and suddenly the confidence was flying. Predominantly a home-grown team were playing fantastic football. Then it snowballed from there. We could do no wrong.

You have to give a lot of credit to Bruce Rioch and you have to look at Willie Maddren who brought the nucleus of that team together and got very close to making it tick. Then Rioch took over and everything clicked and got us playing great football. I still say that the football played between 1986 and 1988 was some of the finest that anybody in Middlesbrough will have seen. The players we've got now have played some fantastic football, but take Juninho out of the scenario and I think you'll have seen some equally good play during that period.

Bruce's philosophy will always be, 'get the ball down and play'. It's enjoyable to play that way, just ask the players. You can launch it like Wimbledon did, but if you ask a player how he likes to play football they'll always say 'get it down on the deck, pass it and entertain the crowd'. Most fans prefer it that way as well."

You lost your place towards the end of that Third Division season, why was that?

"It was tactical. We'd lost our way a little bit. I wasn't playing that well and we needed to win games. We'd lost or drawn a few and it was getting tight towards the end of the season. My position was midfield, I used to sit and play the anchor man role. Get it, give it, win a few challenges, keep things organised and compact. So dropping me was the easiest option, because if you take me out, we're not playing so defensively. They put Lee Turnbull in, a local striker who scored a few important goals and did well for us before moving to Aston Villa."

After that season it seemed that whenever you got back in, and Boro lost, you were dropped.

"I had my fall outs with Bruce Rioch, I always felt he didn't like me and I didn't particularly like him. But I have to say that at times I didn't play very well. Quite often I was struggling with my back after that major operation. I had trouble with my form and confidence and I was getting stick from the fans. It was hard going onto the pitch knowing that some of them wanted to see you fail, which hurt, because I'm from the area. Eventually I felt like I'd turned it round. When we got into the First Division we went on a pre-season trip to Sweden. Bruce didn't go on that trip, Colin Todd took us. I came back from Sweden top scorer, I was flying, my confidence was good and I was playing really well. Something had happened, I wasn't too concerned about everything, I wasn't too intense about football, I was just enjoying myself. Eventually I got into the side but I should have been in much earlier that year. It was such an honour for me personally to play in the First Division. It was what I'd set out in football to do, and to play well, which I did, was brilliant. I was at a level of football which I'd always felt I could play at and I was proving it to myself and a lot of other people. I was really enjoying myself, when unfortunately, I broke my leg. The injury wasn't particularly bad, a six to eight weeks job, but it was towards the end of the season, we were struggling again to avoid relegation. From Bruce's point of view it was a player that he didn't really rate that highly, proving him wrong, and doing a job for him. From my point of view I'd worked my behind off to get in that position - then to have it taken away from me was one of the lowest points of my life."

Yes, after being out of the first team for the best part of two seasons, to come back and play like that, then have it taken away must have been heartbreaking?

"It killed me, I cried for days, I was inconsolable. Even Bruce's attitude towards me changed after that. He started to get interested and show a bit more respect, which I appreciated. I saw him when he came back here with Arsenal, it was 'how are you? Great to see you.' I suppose there's no bitterness and I do respect the fella even though he made things difficult for me."

How would you describe Bruce Rioch as a manager?

"Bruce modelled himself on Cloughie. When we were in hotels for away games he'd get us together and have a massive drinking session. All he'd talk about was football. It was 'Cloughie this and Cloughie that'. He'd talk about playing with Toddy at Derby; it was alright for the first two and a half hours! Being young lads we'd want to talk about other things, but that was Bruce. It all added to the team spirit, getting pissed together, the wind ups, then running it off in training."

Was there one big fall out or was it a gradual process?

"We nearly came to blows on one occasion. But it's the past, it's gone. I'll always say I like Bruce despite everything that's gone on before. Deep down he probably thinks differently of me now than he did then as a player. I didn't help myself a lot of the time, I probably should have had my hair shorter, I probably should have shaved a few more times. Colin Todd always used to like me. He was always pushing to get me into the side. In that First Division period it was Toddy who got me into the team. He pulled me to one side and said, 'Look, it's taken me ages to get you in. Do yourself justice.'"

Is there one reason above all others why Boro were relegated in 1989?

"There weren't enough players. Bruce had been very fortunate in the previous two years because we didn't have that many injuries. But that season Gary Hamilton got crocked, I got injured, and when we went to Sheffield Wednesday for the last game of that season there were six or seven of us on crutches! I remember someone at Wednesday saying, 'If we can't beat these, who can we beat?' We barely got a squad out that day. I think Bruce was very wary about who he bought. He didn't want anyone who might threaten his authority. He needed younger lads who he could manipulate and rule with an iron fist. When he brought in Peter Davenport, who'd been to Forest and Manchester United, he couldn't talk to him like he could the rest of the lads. There was conflict between Bruce and 'Davvy' very early in their relationship, due to Bruce's manner and Peter not accepting it. I think in hindsight 'Davvy' was probably right. So Bruce had a problem with who he could sign, who was going to upset the dressing room, make the lads see what goes on at other clubs or put 'bad ideas' in their heads. As a result, he didn't sign anybody. But there was money there and he needed to sign players. We should never have gone down that season. We were far too good a side, just like the 1997 season."

A lot of people at the time put the blame for relegation on Peter Davenport because his signing created such expectations. Then, when the goals didn't come, the morale of the team seemed to ebb away.

"There could be a little bit of truth in that. I'll never blame Peter Davenport, because when Peter came to the club I thought he played very well without scoring goals. Then he didn't play very well, and still didn't score any goals! That was the problem. I don't think Peter and Bernie Slaven got on very well, Bernie was scoring as he always did, but I don't think he ever linked-up that well with 'Davvy'. What you've got to remember as well is that Peter started off as a central striker and ended up being played out on the left flank. You're not going to get many goals from there. From the club's point of view it didn't turn out to be a good signing, but it needn't have been like that. I'll always think that Peter was a very good footballer."

Why did you sign for Darlington?

"They wanted me. At that time Bruce Rioch and I were finished; there's a whole host of things I could tell you. I ended up being suspended from the club for a couple of weeks. Basically that was wrong, Bruce was totally out of order in what he was doing and I got the PFA involved. I knew Brian Little from his days as reserve team coach at Boro, and he was great for me. He gave me confidence. I didn't need to go to the Vauxhall Conference, there were other clubs in the (then) Second Division after me.

I had the chance to go to Scunthorpe. They offered £100,000 plus, but I turned it down. Bruce more or less told me I would be going somewhere. I said I'd go where I wanted when I wanted, because I wouldn't have anyone dictate to me like that. I'd been seven or eight years at the club, and if I was going to be kicked out, I might as well be kicked out to where I wanted.

I didn't want to move anyway. I had a meeting with Bruce and the chairman and told them I wanted a free transfer. It was funny that I could have got a free transfer to virtually anywhere, but because I went to Darlington they had to pay £40,000 for me. So I missed out financially because I could have made a lot of money on a free transfer. I could have gone back to Scunthorpe and said, 'you can have me on a free, what are you going to give me?' I went to Brian because money was never an issue with me. I needed someone to put their arm round me and say, 'Go and enjoy yourself.' Because mentally and physically I wasn't having a good time. So I went to Darlington and got injured first game. [Laughs]"

Was that the injury that caused your eventual retirement?

"No. That was a knee ligament and cartilage injury. My first game for Darlington was as sub against Chorley, which we won. The next game was at Barrow on a wet and windy New Year's Day, I'd just been in the worst hotel ever and I thought 'What am I doing here?' I started the game, then just before half time, a lad caught me with a beauty and I was out for another four months. I got back in April and got my medal for getting promoted from the Conference, but I had no part in that. The following season was a lot better. We got promoted from the Fourth Division and I left when we were getting relegated from the Third Division the following season.

It seemed everywhere I went it was either promotion or relegation, or both. In the whole time I was at Middlesbrough, there was only one season when we weren't either relegated or promoted. At Darlington it was promotion, promotion, relegation. That one season at Darlington, 1990-91, was fantastic. Again, if you ask the Darlington fans, I don't think they'll ever see any better football than they saw that season."

Could you tell then that Brian Little would go a long way?

"Yes, he had the ability to put his arm round you and make you think he meant it, even if he didn't. That's man management. I always felt Brian would do well. He learned a lot from Bruce Rioch I thought. In his coaching, his knowledge of the game, and tactically, Rioch was second to none in my opinion. He should be in charge of the Scottish national team. What's always let him down, if you look at the clubs he's been to, is that he's had problems with certain players. He hasn't got the ability to accept, or maybe he has now, that not everyone is regimented and military. Some

people have a little bit of spirit which makes them the player they are. Bruce's man-management tended to let him down a little bit. That's where Colin Todd used to fit in. He was a master at making the lads laugh, being one of the boys, and making the dressing room a nicer place to be."

What do you think of the switch from relying on local talent to importing expensive foreigners?

"I think it's got out of hand in the Premiership and I think it will be to the detriment of the national team eventually. It seems to me that we won't be able to produce enough players. But for Middlesbrough, I'm all for it. Juninho is the finest player I've ever seen; no one will ever see a better footballer than him. He's the Wilf Mannion of our era. We'll be telling our kids and grandkids about the little Brazilian that came to Middlesbrough.

You watch him and you think, you can't play football like that in the top flight in England; you play like that in school yards. I'm all for the policy of bringing players in if they are the right players. It lifts the club and the area. The press weren't happy though. They slaughtered the club for no other reason than the fact that Boro had the audacity to go and buy some good players. Who are Middlesbrough to go and do that?

If you look at the foreign players, Juninho's out there by himself. Ravanelli did a good job, you couldn't fault his goalscoring, but he upset the dressing room. I don't like to see a player moaning at his team mates all the time. From time to time if he didn't get the ball he wanted, he was gesticulating as if to say, 'you shouldn't be on the same pitch as me'. You could argue that it showed he cared of course. He could have thought, 'I'm getting £40,000 a week, who cares?' But I remember when he toned it down and started encouraging his team mates, the team visibly played better."

When we signed Juninho the London Evening Standard ran an article saying Middlesbrough was an industrial wasteland, you can't see anything but slagheaps. They even said the women are ugly, all because Juninho signed for us rather than Arsenal.

"I'll beg to differ on the women front! I was starting to feel protective. I've never been one to go around saying Middlesbrough's this or Cleveland's that. I've always had my pride and I don't need to express it to anybody, but when you hear all that stuff, you think wait a second, what's happening? It's just the arrogance that a lot of people still have about the North. I see a lot of press people through my work and some of them are the scum of the earth. They don't care about football at all. They're looking for a story, always to the detriment of the person involved, or anything he's about. They're always looking for another angle."

They're always after negatives.

"Always. That's why I would have loved to see Boro stay up in 1997. Forget the Cups. I would have loved to have said to the other Premiership sides, 'There you go lads, we're still there, and we're going to challenge next season'. I'm sure Boro would have challenged if we'd stayed up. It's disappointing because it put the club back three years, but relegation was better for Boro in the long run."

Do you think it was a mistake getting rid of players like Paul Wilkinson and John Hendrie earlier in the 1996-1997 season?

"It's easy to say with hindsight, but yes. John Hendrie would have done a job, Wilko as well. At the end of the season we were short. I also think we should have played with two up front. We needed to win games. Certainly at Leeds for the last game, we had Chris Freestone on the bench. He needed to be on, Leeds were there for the taking. You could see in the first ten minutes that they didn't want to know. So if we'd scored first they would have thrown the towel in. Instead we went for the other option, keep it nil-nil then see if we could sneak a goal through Juninho. As it happened, Brian Deane scored and we got one back, but we couldn't force the winner. But it's easy to say with hindsight."

We had so many chances to save ourselves right up to the last minute, especially the penalty that wasn't given at Blackburn.

"I was fuming after that. The little fella's been brought down, everyone in the ground has seen it - surely it was a penalty. We saw some terrible refereeing displays during the season, but that was blatant. Does his leg have to come off before it's given? It was infuriating because Juninho's not a cheat; he doesn't dive about. Even if he did it was still a penalty. I remember thinking at the time that's the difference between a side that's going to go down, and one that'll stay up, and it was that one decision."

You played in some big games at Ayresome Park. How does it compare to the Riverside for atmosphere?

"The Riverside is unbelievable. You could get 25,000 or 30,000 in Ayresome Park for a night game and you'd have a fantastic atmosphere, but compared to the Cellnet... There must be something in the design to make sure the sound reverberates around."

The roof channels all the sound. At touchline level it can be deafening.

"The only time I've heard anything like it was the lads walking out at Wembley for the Coca Cola Cup Final. That was a goosepimple job. But week in week out the atmosphere is superb."

Do you think there was tso much difference in ability between Juninho, Ravanelli and Emerson and the other players in the team?

"No I don't. I think Ravanelli thought so. Look at Craig Hignett, the much maligned Craig Hignett. I've always rated Higgy, look at the way he played with Juninho. People say he couldn't tackle, but he's not that kind of player. He's creative, he scores goals, and sets up chances. Other players tackle and win the ball - that's why you have a team.

I think Robbie Mustoe was a fine player in the role he had. I think he was a better team player than Emerson. Not individually, he didn't have the skill of Emerson, but if I was picking that team to play week in, week out, Mustoe would have been one of the first names on the sheet. You always knew what you were going to get. Honest, tackled well, kept it simple, and very rarely gave the ball away, which is very important. There's possibly some players who weren't up to playing in the Premiership, but you can't buy eleven Juninhos."

Whenever anyone talks about the team of '86, '87, '88, it's always said that what made Boro succeed was team spirit. Was it that crucial?

"Our team spirit was fantastic, I've never played anywhere where it's been better. It was special, the lads all got on. The crack in the dressing room was the funniest you'll ever come across. Gary Hamilton was a legend for me. Hammy was the funniest man ever, ruthless beyond belief. Stuart Ripley, Pally [Gary Pallister], Mogga [Tony Mowbray], all great lads. You can't fault them.

We all wanted to win, we all had a common cause. No one was getting that much money, I think Pally had just signed a good contract, Mogga was looked after - but no one was getting anything like what the lads are getting now. It was a pride thing. A load of young lads doing what they did best and doing everyone proud in the process."

Manchester City's Asa Hartford [left] looks on as Billy Ashcroft gets stuck in

Billy Ashcroft

illy Ashcroft was Middlesbrough's first six-figure signing. John Neal returned to his former club Wrexham to sign the Liverpool born striker in 1977. Despite scoring on his home debut, he is probably best remembered for his performances at centre back, following the departure to Newcastle of Stuart Boam. His career spanned Boro's decline from established top division club, through the cup quarter-final defeats in 1978 and 1981, to relegation in 1982. He was released by manager Bobby Murdoch after relegation, and moved to Twente Enschede in Holland, where he became a cult hero impersonating Tommy Cooper on TV, and judging talent contests. Now running a pub in Southport, Billy was happy to reminisce about some of the happiest days of his career.

John Neal was your manager at Boro. He also signed you for Wrexham at the start of your career, he obviously rated you highly?

"Yes, I was spotted by a bloke called Jack Daniels playing my fifth ever game of football. John Neal told me that there would be a job for me at Wrexham when I finished school, so the Monday morning after I left I turned up at Wrexham, but John had forgotten all about it. He was as good as his word in the end because I was there for the next ten years!"

You also played in Europe for Wrexham?

"Yes, a couple of times, Anderlecht, FC Zurich plus various Polish and Swedish teams. We were never knocked out in the First Round. We were a good footballing side; Mickey Thomas and Joey Jones were in the team then."

How did the 'Bear of Brussels' nickname come about?

"I think something was lost in the translation, it was 'The Aardvark' or something similar originally. We played Anderlecht and I was really wound up. I was two feet higher than the keeper going for crosses, bundling him into the back of the net. I went down a storm, and at the time, I looked like Mungo Jerry with the hair and the sidies. When we came back the newspapers were full of the Bear of Brussels thing. Anderlecht tried to buy me six weeks later. John Neal said I was too young to go, so they signed Duncan McKenzie instead. Crap replacement. [Laughs]"

And a totally different player to you.

"I think they thought all English centre forwards were the same. Duncan played like a Belgian, full of skill. They wanted a battering ram; Duncan went over there with his ballet tights on. But the money they were offering was ridiculous, my eyes lit up. When John told me I wasn't going he put my wages up to £68 a week - thanks very much! But he looked after me, I can't complain. At Wrexham the players had no idea what each other earned. You'd go into John Neal's office, which was like a sauna; he chain-smoked and you couldn't understand his Geordie accent. So you didn't know what you were getting until you saw your wage packet. He used to con us all. One lad said he went to see John about a contract extension and came out with less! John was a brilliant fella though."

You grew up as an Everton fan?

"I still am. All the family are Evertonians. When I scored the only goal for Boro against Everton my Dad wouldn't speak to me. I hit it from thirty-five yards; it bounced four times and beat George Wood. My Dad did his nut. He said, 'You played against Liverpool the other week and you were shite!' We went to the pub and he wouldn't let me sit at the same table, but I had Liverpool fans buying me beer all night."

When John Neal went to manage Boro did you know he'd be taking you with him?

"I had an inkling. We were neighbours, so I saw a lot of him. He used to let things slip like, 'I'd love you to sign for Middlesbrough.' I didn't sign a new contract with Wrexham because I knew I'd double or treble my wages going to Middlesbrough, plus there would be signing on fees. Unfortunately I broke down on the way to join Boro - I turned up for the meeting with Charles Amer late and covered in oil. I loved the media attention. I remember wearing a really bad suit, great big collars and a kipper tie. I think I was Boro's first six-figure signing, £135,000. I was the Ravanelli of the day, the 'Red Feather'. The fee was actually £120,000, which they raised to £135,000 so I could get a cut. I'd never had that much money in my life. I knew I was in the First Division."

There's a lot of talk now about the gap between the Premiership and the rest. Did you notice a big gap in moving up to the old First Division?

"Personally yes. At Wrexham the style of play was built around the players we had available. Mickey Thomas would put crosses in, if I couldn't get a header on goal I'd knock people out of the way for Bobby Shinton or Graham Whittle to score. At Middlesbrough it was all about playing in the channels, which wasn't my game at all, so I had to adjust. It was difficult to change after being an out and out striker for ten years. Probably my best time at Boro was when I moved back to centre-half."

It seems strange to try and stop a player doing what he's best at.

"It's like Tony Adams; when he played for Arsenal he hoofed the ball away. When he played for England he was expected to play football and bring the ball out. If that's what they want, play Rio Ferdinand. I had two decent years at the back because I was competent on the ball. I could win it and play it through midfield."

Were you surprised when John Neal asked you to switch?

"No, because I'd done it before. I'd played full-back and midfield. One month I played right-back and marked Peter Barnes, the following week I marked John Robertson [Nottingham Forest], then I was in midfield marking Liam Brady against Arsenal. That's not bad for a six foot two, fifteen stone centre-forward. Forest beat us, Robertson got two including a penalty, but he didn't really do that well! I did okay in the other two games too, so John knew I could defend. My biggest compliment was when Boamy was sold. He was probably the best out-and-out centre half in the First Division - apart from people like Lawrenson and Hansen."

People talk about the quality of the Premiership with all the imports, but some of the players you've just mentioned in the First Division twenty years ago, Brady, Robertson, Hansen and Worthington were every bit as good weren't they?

"Liam Brady was probably one of the best midfield players ever. Souness was great at Boro, but he found another dimension at Liverpool. Dalglish, people like that, great, great players. I don't think the quality is any better today, it's just quicker. People think quicker. Diets are better, I wouldn't have lasted five minutes. Imagine not having a pint after the game? If I had an argument with Tony McAndrew on the pitch, we wouldn't go home and sulk about it. We went down the pub and after a few pints, he would tell me I'd been shite or whatever. Over a pint we'd sort it out. That was where we resolved things."

Without being disrespectful, like pub teams do?

"I've said it many times, we were one of the better pub teams. Liverpool were a pub team. They all lived in the same area, they'd go out and discuss tactics. I found the same thing when I played in Holland. One of my best friends there was Jan Sorenson, who was Walsall manager in 1998. We used to have a pint and a game of darts on Wednesday night and talk about tactics for Sunday. Then we'd go in on Thursday, have a pint with the trainer, then tell him what we thought we should be doing on Sunday. If we didn't fancy training that was okay, as long as we turned it on match days. I was second top scorer in Holland that season with thirty-three goals. In the end three of us picked the team over a pint!"

How did you end up in Holland?

"When I found out that Boro's manager, Bobby Murdoch, was releasing me, Heine Otto took a video to Holland. Apparently the deciding factor was the Boro-Villa game in November 1981 where we were losing three-one with twelve minutes left - I came on and scored twice and they showed about three minutes on Match of the Day. My goals only filled about twenty seconds but Heine showed the video to the chairman of FC Twente, and on the basis of what Heine had already told them, they signed me on a ridiculous wage and I had three great years there. Although we were relegated in the first year, once the dead wood had been cleared out and the club hired a new coach, things improved and we came second the following season to get promoted again."

Was training different at FC Twente?

"I thought we trained hard at Boro. But on Tuesdays at Twente we did eighteen, two-hundred metre sprints with twenty seconds between each one. I was on my knees after the first time. Then we did eighteen, four-hundred metre sprints with thirty seconds between each one. But after a few weeks of this I felt absolutely brilliant and had lost a stone in weight. My game improved leaps and bounds too because apart from Tuesdays everything else was done with the ball. We called it Tommy Cooper day, because at the end of all that running, everyone sounded like Tommy Cooper. Plus it was total football, if the sweeper came up into attack, I'd drop back and cover. You could play in a number of positions and there would always be someone covering for you. I loved it."

So you were always flexible?

"Yeah, except for my knees. [Laughs] I can't understand why we don't do it here. Centre-forwards quite often play centre half when they're older, why not do it during games anyway. It's a great way of doing things."

Dutch is a very difficult language to speak, did you have problems in that respect?

"Scousers are very gregarious, I didn't have any problems. I was introduced to a guy who owned a clothing factory when I'd been there four days. I ingratiated myself to the point where I gave him £5,000 and he bought me a £25,000 Mercedes 280! He got three other blokes to sponsor it with him. My petrol and insurance were paid. I asked if he wanted his name on the car. He said, 'It's a bloody Mercedes, not a Ford.' They did it for the sake of friendship. None of my family ever had to buy a pair of jeans either, he gave us stuff from the factory. We still keep in touch now."

How did you become famous for doing Tommy Cooper impressions?

"I was in a pub in Liverpool the day before I was getting married and a friend of mine, who was a comedian, walked in doing Tommy Cooper - right behind him was the real Tommy Cooper! I spent the day with him, and then he asked if I could give him a lift home. I said 'okay' thinking he'd be at The Adelphi. It turned out to be Chiswick in West London. We drove down there in ten hours due to fog, and by the time we got there all three of us were doing Tommy Cooper. When I was in Holland I started doing it for the lads on a night out. They loved it so much that one of them told a TV programme about it. The next thing I was doing it as a live link on TV. We're not frightened to do anything in Liverpool, and they loved that. When I went to away grounds after I'd done Tommy Cooper on TV if there was a pause in play I could see the fans offering me bottles of beer and

1979 – Billy Ashcroft and Peter Johnson at White Hart Lane with Tottenham's Chris Jones

fags or shouting out requests. The coach didn't mind because I was scoring left right and centre. I got phone calls from universities asking me to go and do a Tommy Cooper show. They were offering around £800 for an hour spot. The coach didn't want me to do it though, so I didn't do it."

You were also judging talent contests in Holland.
"I didn't want to be a judge, I wanted to get my guitar and start singing. It was like being a celebrity, which was one of the great things about it. I had a great time in Holland."

You must have missed all that when you came back to Tranmere.
"My darkest days were playing for Tranmere. No fault of theirs, but I had a nightmare. I did all the pre-season, then on the day of the first game we had a warm up at the ground, I slipped, banged my head and ricked my neck. I got concussion which I guess was one of my highlights at Tranmere! It was all downhill from there. I only played about fifteen games. At the end of the season Frank Worthington didn't renew my contract so I decided it really was time to retire. I've got a trapped nerve in my back and plastic in my face from Wrexham and Holland."

How did that happen?
"Someone butted me when I was at Wrexham."

Deliberately?
"I'd like to think not. Neil Adams it was – he's still in the black book! But as I got older it was taking me thirty minutes to warm up for training compared to fifteen and my body knew it was time to pack it in. Then I had to get a proper job."

Is that when you went into the pub trade?
"I had a year off first before writing to a couple of companies. Whitbreads are the top company to work for and I've been working for them thirteen years."

Is there one highlight of your time at Boro?
"With the exception of relegation everything was a highlight. From making my debut to the day I left. I was at Wrexham for ten years, in Holland for three, and although I enjoyed being at those clubs, The Boro is a special place for me. It's difficult to put into words, but being with the likes of Graeme Hedley, Alan Ramage and Tony McAndrew, three of my best mates, it was a magic place to be. The supporters are probably the best in the country too. It's great because they all remember me. They come in

to my pub and bring me little presents, like my Juninho scarf. I did the half-time draw at the Wrexham-Boro game a few years back. I gave the Wrexham end a wave and got a round of applause - I went to the Boro end and the reception they gave me made the hairs on the back of my neck stand up. It was absolutely brilliant."

Were you there for the last game at Ayresome Park?

"Yeah, that was emotional. Again the noise when my name was announced was amazing. I played at The Riverside in the game before Bernie Slaven's testimonial but I'd love to be playing there now. Not for the money, to be back with the lads I suppose."

When you were at the club Boro had the makings of a great side with players like Souness, Proctor, Hodgson, and Armstrong. Did you see relegation coming when those players were sold?

"I saw it coming before the season started. That's why I wasn't in the team. We went to Scotland pre-season, there was no pattern and nobody knew what they were doing. I mentioned it to Bobby Murdoch; he threw a cup at me - I didn't start the season. Bob was a great coach, we got on great, but I don't think he was a manager. He couldn't cajole players like John Neal could and he didn't have a sidekick to help him."

He probably hasn't got the credit he deserves for the players he brought through as a coach.

"Absolutely, a fabulous coach. I was disappointed when he released me but I've got no axe to grind."

What's the story about you scoring a forty-yarder with a hangover?

"It hadn't developed into a hangover, at that stage I was still pissed... or merry shall we say. I was best man for Bob Scott who played for Hartlepool. John Neal rested me because I wasn't playing well at the time so I wasn't expecting to play at all. I'd had half a bottle of rum, four pints and I got the missus to drop me at Ayresome Park. When I got there Craig Johnston had turned an ankle, David Hodgson had broken a stiletto and Mark Proctor lost his make up. [Laughs] So I had to go on the bench. Then I had to come on with ten minutes left.

Kenny Sansom told me I smelt like a brewery. As he said it Jim Platt hoofed the ball up field which bounced just over my head. I didn't fancy going after it, so I turned and whacked it with my left foot. It flew in the top corner from thirty yards. I couldn't see it after twenty yards, my vision was a bit blurred. As soon as I heard the roar I put my hands up as if I'd meant it. After the game I had to do interviews explaining how I'd played so well, even though I touched the ball about twice. Then it was off to Madison's to celebrate."

It's unfortunate that two of the games that people remember you for are Orient and Wolves in 1978 and 1981, both in the Cup.

"Yeah, and both games it was one lapse of concentration. Having said that Andy Gray who scored for Wolves was a fantastic player. I saw him move one way out of the corner of my eye, I reacted, and he went the other way and scored. Tony McAndrew nearly cut me with his tongue over that one. The other one was the missed chance against Orient. The trouble is it's so long ago I can't remember who else to blame. [Laughs] Ninety-nine times out of hundred I'd have put that away, it's one of those things. The drunken thirty-five-yarder and the Orient miss balance themselves out."

Is there one game you think of as your best for Boro?

" I was never one of the Middlesbrough greats, more a bread and butter player. If I had a good game it was balanced out by the crap games, but one that springs to mind is Birmingham away. We won three-one, I got two. Trevor Francis had just come back from America to play for Birmingham and I remember Dennis Howells, who was Minister for Sport, saying in the 'paper the next day that the England forward line should be Ashcroft and Francis. Not Francis and Ashcroft, Ashcroft and Francis! We had Proctor, Johnston, Armstrong and Hodgson; we destroyed a good Birmingham side. That was one of the best footballing sides Boro have had for a long time."

When you were at Ayresome Park was it a case of Boro simply being happy to be in the First Division?

"Once you're happy to be where you are ambition stops. John Codington, our coach, had a great saying: "If you aim for the ceiling you'll only get halfway up the wall. If you aim for the sky you'll get to the ceiling."

I didn't realise what he meant until the 1980-1981 season, when we finished in mid-table. We got complacent and were relegated next season. We should have set our sights far higher. Having said that we always wanted to improve and Tony McAndrew would never settle for second best. He was always ready to put a boot up someone's arse. I could do with him here in the pub some nights!"

Alan Peacock challanges Brentford's goalie Chic Brodie during Boro's 1964 2-1 FA Cup defeat

Alan Peacock

Alan Peacock was an England centre-forward who is best remembered as part of Boro's home grown forward line of the late 1950's which consisted of Day, Holliday, Clough, Peacock, and McLean. Despite this fire power the club remained in the Second Division due to the large amount of goals conceded. Alan Peacock came up through the youth and schoolboy ranks and made his debut in 1955-56. Tall and good in the air, he was the perfect partner for the prolific Brian Clough. Following Clough's departure to Sunderland in 1961, Peacock came into his own as a goal scorer as well as a provider. In his last two full seasons 1961-62 and 1962-63, he scored twenty-four and thirty-one goals respectively. Frustrated by the clubs lack of ambition, and inability to get out of the Second Division; he left to join Leeds in 1964. He was part of the Leeds team which lost the 1965 F.A. Cup Final to Liverpool. He gained six England caps, and made his debut in the 1962 World Cup in Chile. He retired due to a knee injury in 1968, and is now a match day host at the Riverside Stadium.

How has the game changed since you played?

"It's changed beyond all recognition."

Are the changes for better or worse in your opinion?

"Commercially for the better. I'd love to play at the Riverside now. George Hardwick told me recently that he thought the game now is made for me. I was a thinker and a runner, if you make the right runs, you'll get the balls if you've got players good enough to give you it. Because the game was slower when I played players had more time on the ball and there was more skill.

They've just re-laid the pitch at The Riverside because it was in a terrible condition, but we used to play in mud that came over the top of your boots! The ball was heavy, the shirts used to soak up rain like a wooly cardigan, the boots were leather so they soaked up all the rain. Everything was heavy making the game much slower.

Players throw the ball into the box now but in our day sometimes you couldn't even kick it from the corner flag to the far post. When the keeper took goal kicks, if you were a centre forward, you'd stand on the edge of the box because he'd struggle to get it over your head. It was also more physical, Cloughie was finished at twenty-eight; me at twenty-nine."

What was the injury?

"Cruciate ligaments, but I've done the lot. I got the injury in my first year at Leeds, just after we got promoted. We were playing over in Berlin against the East German national side and Don Revie had decided to buy Allan Clarke to play alongside me.

There was no insurance then, so they fixed up a transfer to Plymouth. Leeds gave them some money and they gave some to me. I was there about three months when a specialist told me that if I was injured again I'd end up a cripple - so I packed up. Then Cloughie tried to sign me when he was at Derby, he wanted to play me at the back with Roy McFarland as I'd played both centre-half and wing-half at Middlesbrough."

Who was the most physical opponent you ever came across?

"I was playing for Micky Fenton in the reserves, I can't remember if it was against North Shields or South Shields but their centre half was an ex-Newcastle player called Frank Brennan, a big strong bloke and a good player. Of course he was finished then, but I was sixteen and dead keen, so I gave him the run around. The ball was crossed in, I went up and flicked it on, then the next thing I knew something hit me. I thought I'd broken my jaw, I was spitting teeth out. Micky Fenton came running on, gave me a rub with the sponge and said I'd be alright.

We played them again a few days later at Ayresome Park and Micky said, 'Just go and hit him. When he goes up dig him just under the ribs.' When the ball came over I got him with my elbow as hard as I could but he just headed the ball away. I thought, 'Jesus, you're in trouble now!'

He never bothered me until we got a corner. Everyone was watching Billy Day take the kick when Frank stamped on my toes. Back then our boots had steel toecaps, but he's stamped so hard that the steel went into my toes. When they got the boot off they had to hammer the toecap back into place before I could go back on. I'm glad I only played against him twice!"

What league did the reserves play in?

"The Wearside League. You'd get ex-pros from Boro, Newcastle, Sunderland, Darlington and Hartlepool because the colliery teams in that league would give them a job at Easington or Seaham plus £6 or £7 a match. Combined they were earning more than we were getting as pros! We'd go to some places where they didn't half dish it out. It was a bloody hard league.

Before you got to the first team you'd play in the Northern Intermediate League and the North Eastern League, as well as the Wearside League. It was a steady progression, and a very good upbringing. But once players made it into the first team the coaching stopped.

When I went to Leeds we often went back in the afternoon and tried different moves, working on things after normal training. That was the professional attitude that was missing at Middlesbrough. Boro was a good club, but it wasn't professional; you just went out and you played. Very little tactics. You just played to your position in the two-three-five system. Two full backs, three wing halfs, five forwards, with the inside-forwards dropping deep. Later on Cloughie and I played as twin centre-forwards."

How did you rate Ravanelli as a centre-forward?

"A hat trick on your debut isn't bad. But what I noticed was if he made a run and didn't get the ball, the arms would go up in disgust, if he didn't get the ball on his next run, same again. The third time he wouldn't run. I loved watching Juninho, but I kept thinking what a waste of talent. There was nobody running for him; creating space for him to go into. If you make a run and take a defender you've left a hole. If the defender doesn't go with you, Juninho would give you the ball. A lot of the time Juninho had the ball without many options, so he'd beat one man, but eventually the third or fourth would get him. He needed players running off him."

You played for Boro at a time when they were marooned in the Second Division. Why do you think the club didn't achieve promotion when you played?

"If the right people had been at the club the potential might have been realised. At that time Liverpool were in the Second Division. They'd bought in Ian St. John, who told me that Bill Shankly came in for me too. We were every bit as good as that Liverpool side, but they bought players and went forward - we just sold players.

If you imagine our forward line of Day, Holliday, Clough, McLean and Peacock at Boro now, the club would buy big to build around those players and let them develop from there. But Middlesbrough never bought the right players. They would buy men who were finished; who wanted a club to give them one last contract. There was no ambition. The ambition had to come from yourself.

So at the time I was there, there was nothing happening. It was smashing for me because I was a local lad, but you'd never get a Cup run. We got Manchester United in the Third Round in January 1961 and they beat us three-nil at Old Trafford - that was a big game. But even with Brian Clough, Eddie Holliday, Billy Day, good players, the best we finished was fourth in the Second Division."

Was the club just lucky that yourself, Clough, Day, Holliday and McLean all came through at the same time?

"No, the youth system at Middlesbrough was super. Look at the ex-players who were running that system. Johnny Spuhler and George Hardwick ran the junior and B League teams, Jimmy Gordon ran the Northern Intermediate League team, George Camsell ran the A team which was between the junior and the reserve teams, and Micky Fenton ran the reserves. You mentioned just five, but players like Mick McNeil, Cyril Knowles and Gordon Jones also came through that system.

The difference between now and then is that I didn't even have a ball as a kid; we made them out of paper and nylon stockings. All we did was play football, there was nothing else. I used to go and see Mannion and Fenton, people like that for sixpence. Now if you want to take your family it's bloody expensive. When I was at school in North Ormesby, there were five or six schools. They all had a team and a reserve team.

What happens now is that all the kids go to a comprehensive school and you've got one team. What happens to the kids that develop late, because school teams are dominated by big lads? Unless these kids go to the Academy that the club runs you could lose all that talent."

It must be very difficult to predict how different lads will develop.

"You hear people in the pub saying, 'so-and-so's crap. This lad in our Sunday team's a better player.' In that league he may be a good player, but everybody reaches their own level, which is determined by the speed of the game, control of the ball, and your vision. The higher you go the better service you get. If you play with top class players they get the ball and ping it at you quickly, so that gives you a yard. You've seen it coming so that gives you another yard.

In the Second Division the ball doesn't come as quick, and the bloke isn't as quick to receive it. It slows the game down and gives the other players a chance. The good players always have this half a yard because their vision and control is good. What happens is, you come through schools football, local league football, non league, and the quality gets higher and higher, until you find the level that you're good at and you never go any higher."

You made your England debut in the 1962 World Cup in Chile. What prevented you playing before that?

"I was picked twice before the World Cup but I got injured both times. The second injury was six weeks before the twenty-two were picked for the World Cup. I had to get fit and play within that time. It was a fractured cheekbone, and I played within two weeks, which was ridiculous.

The surgeon said it was a six-week job. I said; 'If it goes again can you put it back together?' So I played and got fit and I was taken to the World Cup in Chile. I was unlucky to have got injured in the Bulgaria match because I would have played against Brazil; but I played against Argentina. Their centre-half was called something like 'The Wild Bull of the Pampas'. He was a killer, but I had a good game and should have scored. I beat the 'keeper but the defender punched the ball out - Bobby Charlton scored the penalty. After that it was one injury after another but I still earned another few caps."

Is that why there's a three-year gap between your caps?

"Yes, plus the fact that there wasn't a lot of games. You'd play the Home Internationals, a couple of friendlies and that would be it. Wilf Mannion only got twenty-six caps. If you played for England in the 1962 World Cup you got £60, if not £30, plus £2 a day spending money. Someone totted up my total wages in my nine years at Middlesbrough. It only came to about £10,000. I got £10 signing on fee and took home £7 after tax. For a long time I was was the most expensive player ever sold by Middlesbrough at £55,000."

Who was in the England squad for that World Cup?

"Jimmy Greaves, Bobby Charlton, Ron Springett, Jimmy Armfield, Don Howe, Peter Swan, Roger Hunt, he was my room mate. Stan Anderson, Bobby Robson and Bobby Moore."

That World Cup gets forgotten about because we won the next one.

"And it was very remote; there was only three thousand people at one game. The place we stayed at was a copper mine six thousand feet above sea level. We lived in huts. It was unbelievable!"

You left Boro to go to Leeds in 1964. Could you see that they were going to be successful when you went there?

"Yes, Reaney, Hunter, Bremner, Giles, Charlton; they were all there. The nucleus of a great side was there and we got to the Cup Final in my first full season where Liverpool beat us in the first extra-time Final."

Is the Cup Final as special for players as everyone says it is?

"I would say so. You weren't allowed to warm up on the pitch. You walked out with your suits on, had a look around, then went and sat in the dressing room, listening to the singing. Then you'd hear 'Abide With Me', your throat would be dry; then you were out of the tunnel and you were hit by the noise of a hundred thousand people."

Did you play many European games for Leeds?

"We had two seasons in Europe and the year I left they got to the Final of the Fairs Cup."

Leeds ended up with a reputation for cynicism and gamesmanship. Was that justified?

"I think so. The old Second Division was a hard League, the game in general was harder. I used to think if the centre-half wasn't kicking me, I wasn't doing my job properly. I think it was a case of kicking our way out of that division, then we'd show them how we could play in the First Division. But when we got in the First Division our reputation had gone before us and teams played with the expectation of a physical game.

I wasn't a physical type of player until I went to Leeds. But there was a lot of talent in that team, even though they could all dish it out. But Liverpool were physical, so were Manchester United. Paddy Crerand, Denis Law, Bill Foulkes, they were all hard men; every team had them. That was the way the game was played."

Do you approve of the way FIFA are trying to clamp down on physical play?

"Yes. There has to be a physical element to the game but there's a lot more pulling and tugging now, whereas before they just kicked you!"

How did you get on with Don Revie?

"Super. He was very professional. He did go over the top at times but he believed in things and he got the team doing what he wanted. His ideal way of playing was like the 1960 Real Madrid v Eintracht Frankfurt European Cup Final. He even changed Leeds colours to all white. His vision was that Leeds would emulate Real Madrid and that's what he set out to achieve. He left Leeds strong. Like Brian Clough, people can say what they want about him but he's done it at the highest level. He took Forest and Derby and won things."

Did he strike you as a manager of the future when you played with him?

"He was always different. [Laughs] Despite what people think we got on very well together. We exchange Christmas cards, I think we've got a lot of respect for each other. I was quite happy playing up front with him."

You've probably been asked this many times but while you were at the club, Brian Clough was made captain. In November 1959, nine players signed a letter to directors asking them to strip him of the title, what do you remember of that?

"Nothing, I was in the Army. I only went to Middlesbrough to play the games. I didn't sign it although I could understand the reasons. I only signed full-time professional when I came out of the Army. That was only a couple of years before Cloughie left. Before the Army I was part-time. Tuesday and Thursday night and night school on Monday, Wednesday and Friday, as well as working at the Cargo Fleet works. It brought it back to me recently because my business partner lives at Winyard, near Sir John Hall. He was telling me Shearer lives there, Jamie Pollock lives there, Merson was there, Mustoe's there. It's as if they're competing to see who has the biggest house. I thought, 'they must have some village team here!'"

Who was the best player you played with at Boro?

"I used to think a lot of Bill Harris [Welsh inside-forward between 1954-65 who was thought to be one of the instigators of the anti-Clough letter]. People talk about the five forwards, but Bill was really another forward, because his passing was so good. I was always worried about what was going on behind him though. He was a good player."

You're still involved with the club on match-days, how did that come about?

"When I was a player I used to see people who had been good pros for Middlesbrough practically have to beg for tickets - I didn't go to Boro for about eighteen years at one stage. Then, when Bryan Robson came, he invited George, Wilf and myself to lunch and asked if we'd like honorary membership at the club. Having said for years that I thought ex-pros weren't treated very well, I could hardly say no. I really enjoy the involvement again, but I must admit when the game starts I'm not the best watcher. I'd rather be out on the pitch."

John Spuhl

1953 – Johnny Spuhler tries to round Charlton goalie Sam Bartram at The Valley

Johnny Spuhler is a player who tends to be overlooked. In the absence of major trophies, Boro's history is usually written in terms of great players. Johnny Spuhler played with two of the greatest, in George Hardwick and Wilf Mannion. Spuhler was born in Sunderland and joined them as a boy. He played for England schoolboys, and was unlucky not to be part of the Sunderland team which won the F.A. Cup in 1937. He played as a guest for Boro during World War Two, and signed as a professional after the War. He made his name as a winger or centre-forward and was an integral part of the Mannion and Hardwick era. He also played in the controversial 1947 F.A. Cup Quarter Final, against Burnley. After Boro were relegated from the First Division in 1954, Spuhler was released and signed for Darlington. After two years at Feethams, which included a famous F.A. Cup victory over Chelsea, he became manager of Shrewsbury. He later returned to the North East, and played on for Spennymoor in the North Eastern League, winning the Northern League Trophy. He also took West Auckland to the final of the F.A. Amateur Cup at Wembley. Although Johnny was almost eighty when I spoke with him and his wife Nancy, his memory was undimmed, and he spoke with great affection about the happiest time of his career.

Where are you from originally?

"I was born in Sunderland and made my debut for them at seventeen against Arsenal at Highbury. I was a winger then and I played against Eddie Hapgood the England captain. I went past him once, but instead of threatening to break my legs as most players would have done back then, he said, 'that was good, do it again'."

Your legs must have been jelly.

"Are you joking? It was great."

As a Sunderland lad and a Sunderland player, how did you end up at Middlesbrough Football Club?

"I signed for Sunderland in 1934, straight from school. I was a school-boy international and stayed with them until the War. I was in and out of the team for the period leading up to the outbreak, competing with a lad called Lenny Dunns for the winger's position. Sunderland won the Cup in 1937. They beat Preston North End three-one, but I missed it and was really upset. Then the War came and changed life completely."

Did you play during the War?

"I was asked if I would play as a guest for Carlisle. I was working night and day in the shipyards, then I used to get a taxi to Carlisle with three other lads. We used to go up there every home game, and do you know how much we got? Ten bob a game. Carlisle was a big troop town and they could get twenty or thirty thousand people in. But all we were getting was ten bob [50p], plus expenses. When the league started up again Sunderland sent me a letter saying 'you are a Sunderland player, you will report for training'. I said no. When the War started we were just kicked out. There was no compensation, no pity, nothing was done for the families.

Mrs. S: "Johnny went to the dole office and they told him he couldn't get any money because football wasn't work, it was a game."

"I was out of work because they wouldn't put me in the forces. I think my name upset them, they thought I was a foreigner. They threatened me with jail because I registered with the Army then joined the Navy, but I ended up working in the shipyards, which was vital work. When the War finished I eventually re-signed for Sunderland. The manager was an old Sunderland full-back called Bill Murray who wasn't very popular. So when David Jack came to the house and asked if I'd like to sign for Boro, I said, 'where's the form?' I signed for £2,000; the biggest fee Middlesbrough had paid in a long time. We were happy in Sunderland, we'd just bought a bun-galow and loved the people, but then we moved to Middlesbrough."

Mrs. S: "We loved Middlesbrough, we had the happiest years of our lives there."

"I liked Sunderland supporters, but to me Middlesbrough supporters had everything. If you had a bad game you were never criticised openly. They'd say, 'never mind, there's another game next week.' They were really nice, open people. We had a club house in Eaton Road for ten years and brought our son and daughter up in Middlesbrough."

What did being a winger entail in your era?

"As a winger your one objective was goals. The one man stopping you scoring goals was the left back, me being an outside-right. If I took command over the full-back I'd give him a hell of a day and I'd get goals. But if he cut me out we were struggling. It was man-to-man right throughout the game."

All over the pitch?

"There was the goalkeeper, two full-backs, three half-backs, you'd call them midfield players today, plus five forwards. You always played with five strikers, two on the wings, one in the centre, and the two who played inside were the inside-right and inside-left. That was what you called a diagonal combination. If you were a winger, the wing half behind you played with you and the inside-forward. It was played in a triangle. They do the same thing now but there's more passes and more mistakes made. With us, it was a three-man pass, and I was away. The idea was to feed the wing-man, get him away, and the inside men got the goals. But it was so simply played. If we were playing Arsenal on Saturday, you could go into any pub in Middlesbrough on Friday night and the main topic would be Middlesbrough playing Arsenal. It would be George Hardwick, our left-back and captain of England, against so-and-so on the wing for Arsenal. Then they talked about our centre-half against their centre-forward. That's what attracted the crowds."

How did the game differ when you played it?

"It was hard but cleaner and tripping was never acceptable. If you tripped a man the referee would have you off. Although every team had a hard man, I don't think I saw more than two men sent off in my career. Jimmy Gordon was called the hard man of Middlesbrough. He was only 5' 8" or so, but he would tackle anything. He wouldn't go in to hurt the man he'd tackle and come out with the ball. Every team seemed to have one. If they tackled you and you moaned they wouldn't like it. But if you said nothing, got up and had another go at him later it was okay. That was what the game was full of, take your punishment, he'll not kill you. If you got criers in the game they were finished. I don't remember seeing more than two really dirty fouls in the whole of my career. As we used to say, 'It's our living'. Why cripple someone and stop him earning his living? They don't think about that now. We were all on the same money. It was £12 per week, then up to £14, and I finished at £16."

Did you feel underpaid?

"We never thought about it because most people were earning £2 per week. If you were on £5 you were in a hell of a job. At seventeen-years-old I was on £12 a week, so it was good money. When I think back, whenever the players had meetings, we never once brought up money."

Was it a good Boro side you came into after the War?

"Yes, we had George Hardwick who was captain of England, plus Wilf Mannion. But you see, when Wilf came back to Middlesbrough after the War he was really out of condition. We thought he'd never play again. He was not up to playing football. He'd put a lot of weight on, but credit to him, he worked hard and gradually it came back to him. I'd known Wilf from schoolboy days, because he'd played in the trials with me and was not selected for England Schoolboys. Can you believe that? I've got a photograph with the Compton brothers in it too. They went on to play football for Arsenal and cricket for England. They couldn't get into the England Schoolboys side though. That's how strong it was. We were undefeated; it was a wonderful team."

The impression you get from reading the reference books is that after the War, the Boro team was made up of just Mannion, Hardwick - plus nine others. Is that a fair reflection?

"Don't you believe it. The people of Middlesbrough, the true supporters, would not stand for that. Sometimes you got frustrated during a game when Wilf would deliberately give you a bad ball. You'd go one way and he knew you'd gone that side, but he'd pass the other way. The crowd couldn't see it but I was sure someone was going to blow. The fella that played behind Wilf was Jimmy Gordon, a fiery Scot. He couldn't stand any of that. I've seen Wilf do that to Jimmy and it took us all to keep Jimmy away from him!"

Why do you think he would give you bad passes?

"No reason at all; five minutes later it was all forgotten. We got on to him, but it was just something inside Wilf. I started to give him bad balls then and he didn't like it. You see he was an idol. He was Middlesbrough born and bred - nothing he did was wrong. But believe me, he was a good player. There's not many as good today. He was like Gazza as a player, but not as a person."

He was that good?
"He was good. He could win games on his own."

Were you still a winger after the War?
"I was moved to centre-forward because Micky Fenton's days were numbered and David Jack had no money to buy anyone. He told me to go into the middle and play as I wanted, which I did. At the time I thought I should have got a cap. I scored goals and provided goals."

Is there one game you think of as your best for Boro?
"I think my best game was against Chelsea."

Mrs. S: "What about the game against Manchester United, when we beat them five-nil in 1953? Tony Thomas was the chairman then. After the game he gave me a cuddle and said he would give me anything in the world. I said take me and the rest of the wives to Wembley for the Cup Final the following week. About ten of the wives decided they wanted to go, so he fixed it. I went to the Cup Final, and the rest of the wives went shopping in London. Then we had a party at night because Boro had beaten Portsmouth four-one."

"That was Lindy Delaphena's return to Portsmouth. He scored a wonderful goal and I got two. With regard to goals my best was when we played Huddersfield at Ayresome Park in 1950; we won eight-nil. That would be my happiest day I think. But the game Nancy's talking about was when Middlesbrough beat Manchester United five-one. That was a case of Wilf Mannion at his best. He didn't say anything, but I knew as soon as he walked onto the pitch Wilf was going to show he was the boss. He put on a terrific exhibition. I've seen Wilf play some wonderful games, but that was his best."

Better than the famous game against Blackpool?
"That's another one they talk about but I wouldn't think Blackpool were in the same class as Manchester United. That Blackpool game was the day Wilf stood in front of their England wing-half, Harry Johnston, and practically took his pants down. He stood on the ball and told them to come and get it. He could do anything. He had the ability, and he didn't care. Mind you, I've got to say this in defence of ourselves, the players - we played forty-two games a season. The Middlesbrough people didn't see Wilf play away. If you'd been watching some of the games away from home, you wouldn't see Wilf."

Someone like a Matt Le Tissier who drifted in and out of games?
"That's the boy. As I said, the man playing behind him, Jimmy Gordon, ran his heart and soul out for Wilf. I've seen him flogged to death, not because Wilf was playing badly, just not putting in what he should. What

can you do? I don't go around abusing other players, if that's the way they want to play the game, fair enough. I couldn't stop them."

Why do you think Boro didn't win anything during your time there?

"I don't know what the reason was, but it wasn't lack of spirit in the team. I wouldn't like to say. The nearest we got to Wembley was when we played Burnley in the Cup Quarter-Final at Ayresome Park. What happened was, Middlesbrough got a free-kick at the Workhouse End, just outside the box. The ball went out of play, I ran off the field and picked it up, because time was getting on. I threw the ball back on to the park, but I didn't go on to the pitch. I stood by the goalpost. Quick as a flash Micky Fenton put the ball down, and hit it into the back of the net. The 'keeper was crafty and claimed to the referee that I was on the field of play and offside, but I obviously wasn't. Of course I got blamed for it, [laughs] and it never died down. We lost the replay at Burnley. Nobody forgave me for that. Micky himself said he should have waited, but that's how I got a bad name - but you live with it."

Who was the biggest character at Boro?

"We had a few. We had a goalkeeper called Ronaldo Ugolini, an Italian-Scot. A wonderful lad, his family had a big fish and chip restaurant in Scotland. We used to go and stay with them. He was a lovely lad, full of fun. In football he was an artist - he wasn't happy to make easy saves. If the ball was going into the corner, he wouldn't just go and get it. He'd wait till the last second, take off, and tip it over the bar. He was a character.

Then we bought a winger from Portsmouth, Lindy Delaphena. He was the first black lad I'd ever met in football and must have been one of the first coloured lads in English football. He replaced me on the wing when I moved into the centre.

Ugolini and Delaphena both liked to be the top man in everything. If we were playing in London we'd get the train down on the Friday. You'd get paid in the morning, do your training, then report to the station. The first time Delaphena came with us he arrived at the station dressed like a film star. He could dress. He came from a well-educated family and I think there was money behind him. We sat down for dinner on the train. He was on the same table as Wilf, Harry Bell and me. The waiter brought the food as usual, and Delaphena asked him what it was. When the waiter said it was dinner, he replied, 'you don't want me to eat trash like that, do you? Take it away and bring me something decent.' I thought 'what have we bought here?' That was his attitude right throughout life.

When we played at Ayresome there was a black supporter who used to go to the games and he was there for about six seasons. He stood in the paddock where we came out. He was a comedian. The ball would go to Delaphena and this voice would come out of the crowd like a foghorn, "YOU BLACK TRASH!" It was great because it put everybody in such good humour. Delaphena used to get worked up and that was what we wanted because when provoked he was brilliant. He could kick like a mule. I'll never forget that fella, he was such a help to the club."

What do you think of the foreign players we have now?
"I admire the little Brazilian. As players, Wilf and him are much the same, except Juninho's faster than Wilf. But it's the money that upsets me. My son lives near Ravanelli. You should see his house and his car. He's supposed to be on £42,000 a week but how does the working public stand for it? As working men, what do the supporters feel about that. They must talk about wages?"

The people I speak to seem to think that if paying fortunes to foreign superstars is the way to get Boro competing at the top, so be it.
"I suppose so."

What was the biggest crowd you played before at Ayresome Park?
"We used to get good gates. The best was a shade under 54,000."

It's incredible to imagine that many people in Ayresome Park. It makes you wonder why the club never had any money.
"The directors did okay. We'd get them travelling with us to London, but when we got to London and had our dinner at night, there would always be guests at their table, all enjoying free meals and tickets to the game. We never had an invitation to take our wives to the match."
Mrs. S: "If I wanted to go I had to go by myself in the car. We went to Sunderland once one or two of the wives. When we got there we were told that there were no spare tickets. I told Johnny, so he had a word with the lads and they said they wouldn't play if we couldn't get tickets. All sorts of hangers-on got tickets and eventually they put us in the Press Box. I can still remember going up the steps and all those blokes saying, 'what's going on?'"

When did you leave Boro?
"It was after relegation in 1954 when I was thirty-seven. When I left Boro I was finished, but I was okay because I had a trade and there was plenty of work in those days. But Darlington offered me a contract. They said they were in a mess and would I give them two years? So I signed as player-coach, and we had a couple of good seasons. We beat Chelsea in the Cup at Feethams, in front of a record crowd before losing in the Quarter-

Final. The manager was Bob Gurney, a centre-forward in the Sunderland Cup Final team. I'd played with him as boy but he didn't like me. I even got the chairman to buy the lads new training gear and he didn't like that either. We had a good team though and were never near the bottom, but it seemed a long two years so I decided to pack it in again."

Didn't you become a Manager?

"I went to Shrewsbury as manager, which was a bad thing. My friend Harry Potts was there, but he was going back to Burnley as manager, so he asked me to take over. I did and it was a big mistake. The team wasn't bad, but there was no money and no connections in the outside world of football. I lodged there for six months, got them out of trouble and into mid-table. Then I told the chairman I'd had enough and I left. That was the last connection I had with professional football."

Did you make a conscious decision to leave football at that stage?

"No, not really. From there I went over to Germany and coached the American forces."

Like George Hardwick?

"He was with us. There were five of us but we never saw each other after the first week. We were given lectures and told where we were going to go. The American soldiers lived in luxury in their big sealed compounds. But they only played American football and those who played it were the top men. They got us in to wipe that out and help develop 'soccer'. I was away about four months, going round the companies. It was a good life, I had a limo, two drivers who were really good fellas.

But it was hard work because finding players was difficult. They were so clumsy, they couldn't do anything with their feet. I was just about finished when I found my first foot regiment. I went into the camp, put my notices up, and found a few lads wanting to play. I had them for three weeks and they were marvellous; natural footballers.

We had a team in no time. Though I say it myself, they were brilliant. The end result was a knockout tournament at HQ. We went there and played George's team in the first leg. We hammered them!

George couldn't believe it. Neither could I. We went on to win the tournament and had a great time."

Was that your last connection with football?

"I went on to manage West Auckland, which was one of the best times of my life because we went to Wembley. We played Walthamstow in the 1961 Amateur Cup Final."

What happened?

"We got beat 2-1. We scored first as well. Our lads were on the floor for the last ten minutes, that's when they got the winner."

What was the crowd?

"About 45,000. They got a new stand and dressing rooms out of the Wembley windfall but the Treasurer disappeared with some of the money. Do you remember the World Cup being stolen from West Auckland?"

I've seen the Dennis Waterman film about it.

"West Auckland won the cup in Italy - legally they were World Champions. Our Chairman, Sid Douthwaite, owned the pub we used to meet in and the cup was in there on display. One day it was stolen and never returned. In the end they had to make a replica."

Did you finish playing when you left Darlington?

"No, Spennymoor in the North Eastern League came along and asked me to give them a couple of seasons as player-manager. The North Eastern League was a big league; Newcastle, Sunderland and Boro reserves all played in it. So I signed for them, got a team together, and in that first season lifted the Northern League Trophy. We beat Sunderland reserves at Roker Park in the deciding game. The people of Spennymoor went crazy."

Was it hard dropping into non-league football?

"Yes and no. You used your loaf, all the knowledge you'd gained. The players would help you out, give a little bit extra for you. I remember Nancy was in the crowd once and someone said, 'look at that old bugger running out, he must be a grandfather by now.' My wife turned round and said, 'He is!'"

Terry Cochrane in typical 'socks round ankles' style against West Brom

Terry Cochrane

Terry Cochrane was an out-and-out winger; the type of player that is rarely seen in the modern game. He was a crowd pleaser, whose game was all about taking on and beating the opposing full-back. It was often said that he wasn't content to beat his man once. He wanted to go back and do it again. Terry was the club record signing when he arrived from Burnley for £238,000 in 1978. A Northern Ireland international, he won nineteen of his twenty-six caps with Boro, and was unlucky not to be part of the Northern Ireland team which made such a big impact in the 1982 World Cup in Spain. He didn't find the net regularly, but a spectacular overhead kick at Swansea in 1980 was captured by the Match of the Day cameras. He was part of the Boro team which got to the F.A. Cup Quarter-Final in 1981, and scored the equaliser against Wolves at Ayresome Park. After relegation in 1982, Malcolm Allison took over as manager and forced out experienced players like Cochrane and his international team mate, Jim Platt. Terry went to Gillingham before returning to Teesside and playing Northern League football for many years.

Is it true that you started out as a central-midfield player?

"Yes, but I was told I was too small to play in midfield, so I went out to the wing. That's where it all took off, from Derry to Linfield, Linfield to Coleraine, Coleraine to Burnley, Burnley to Boro."

Why did you sign for Boro?

"Coming from a small place in Ireland as I did, I didn't know very much. Places in England were just places in England. I'd been at Burnley for three years, and I actually thought I was going to join West Brom. Ron Atkinson had been chasing me for about six months, when one Sunday I got a phone call saying Middlesbrough manager, John Neal, wanted to speak to me.

John took me to the club and showed me around, then gave me a piece of paper and said, 'Will you sign there?' I'd only come to have a look round then all of a sudden I was signing. Being a young lad who didn't know very much, I just signed, but I didn't know that Arsenal wanted me too. But I don't regret signing for Boro. I've made a good life and the fans are brilliant. You'll never get anyone more passionate than you guys."

How important was it that you were a favourite with the fans. Was that something you thought about?

"Very important. I think my reputation was that I was a socialiser and liked a drink and a bet. When you get among the fans and feel the passion, you want to do well for them. I wasn't the best in the world, but I tried."

People always remember you talking to the crowd.

"It's sad that the game has changed so much and nobody does it now. Why not bring a bit of fun into the game?"

You always had the reputation of never being happy to beat your man once, you wanted to do it again.

"Possibly that was my own fault for being arrogant when I played, but I think you've got to have a bit of arrogance. You've got to say 'I'm better than you'. That was the way I played, which you don't see very much anymore. The idea now is to beat you with passes. The game now is all about passing; I don't like that. To get the individual talent, we've got to bring in people from abroad because there's nobody who will do that in England.

Giggs is an individual, but he hasn't done much for a while because the game isn't about that anymore. The classic example is Keith Gillespie. He's got all the pace in the world, but he runs up to his full-back then passes the ball backwards again instead of going past his man and crossing the ball in. But the skill factor will return to the game one day I think, because football's cyclical."

You mean wingers are out of fashion now, but in five years time they might come back?

"I think so."

How did you rate John Neal as a manager?

"John was a quiet man. He wanted to win for Middlesbrough, but in the changing room he wasn't the most exciting person. Not a great motivator. A nice man, but you never got underneath him. He bought me as winger and played me at home, but he didn't want to play me away from home. I wasn't sure what John wanted from me."

Did you feel pressure because you were the club's record signing?

"Not really. Being a daft Irishman I didn't give a damn!"

How good was the Boro side you joined?

"At the time we needed another three or four players, and when I signed John Neal told me they would be brought in. We didn't do too badly though. We weren't the greatest team in the world, but when we went out on a Saturday night we soon knew how the fans thought we'd played. If we were near the bottom of the league some of our lads couldn't go out in town because fans would let their feelings be known.

I think people that play for Middlesbrough should live there so they'll know the passion of the fans and be in contact with them. What the club should do is make the players understand that they're playing for the people of Middlesbrough, because I don't think the imports know that. But when I arrived John Neal said he wanted to make a go of it although we had the 'boring Boro' label for a long time. I see Jack now and again and I love him to bits, but he left that stigma with Boro."

You still had people like David Armstrong, Mark Proctor, Craig Johnston, David Hodgson and Stuart Boam.

"'Spike' [David Armstrong] was a tremendous player. Ian Bailey at left-back, big Ramage at centre-back. I played in the reserves with Alan one Tuesday night against York. There were two lads in the crowd giving 'Ram' so much stick it wasn't true. [Laughs] At full-time he jumped over the fence and took off after them. He chased them right out of Ayresome Park. I also remember beating Wolves 2-0 when Andy Gray was playing for them. During the game he 'did' Ramage. Alan said to him, 'Listen youth,' (he called everyone youth), 'If you do that again I'm going to kill you.' Andy Gray didn't want to know!"

What do you remember about the Wolves Cup Quarter-Final in 1981?

"I thought we were through. I equalised just before half-time. Second-half we should have tied it up, but they were good enough to hold us. But we were still confident going into the replay. I don't think Jankovic's goal was offside. If it had been allowed we'd have done the business. But they beat us after extra-time. What can you say?"

Boro had never been beyond the Quarter-Finals. Was that a factor before the game at Ayresome Park?

"Yes, but I don't think it put any extra pressure on us. We had 34,000 in Ayresome Park against Barnsley in the FA Cup Fifth Round. Having beaten them we thought we were in for the Cup. I really believe that if we'd beaten Wolves then we'd have gone on to beat Spurs, who eventually won the Cup that year. We had big hearts and we would have risen to the occasion."

Did it feel at the time like a turning point for the club, or was it just losing a big game?

"It was just losing a big game. We had a few young players like Craig Johnston, Mark Proctor and David Hodgson, but I thought if we could buy two or three players we would have been a really good side. Don't forget, we finished ninth in the old First Division in 1979-1980, which is not bad for Middlesbrough."

How does the equaliser in the Wolves Quarter-Final game in 1981 rate in the highlights of your career?

"It's one of them. I played a few one-twos, and 'Spike' played me in on the edge of the box. But I think I'm plagued by the Swansea goal; that overhead kick in our five-nil win. It's been with me ever since I scored it. It'll probably never be forgotten by Middlesbrough fans and it's been voted the second best goal in the history of the Boro - I'm over the moon about that. John Hendrie's against Millwall was voted first best but his was a hit and hope job! When we got back from Swansea we were in The Madison and a couple of fans started talking about it."

Did you score a better one?

"I probably scored a better one for Gillingham against Bristol Rovers. The 'keeper knocked it to me and I stopped it and chipped him from the half-way line, like Beckham did. That was voted the best goal ever seen at Gillingham by their fans, but unfortunately there was no Sky TV back then, so nobody else has seen it."

Terry Cochrane challanges for the ball with Nottingham Forest's Archie Gemmill

The perceived view about Bobby Murdoch is that he was a good coach, but not cut out to be a manager - do you agree?

"Bobby was too nice. A lovely man. I think some of the lads he bought didn't play for him. Where he fell down was that he wasn't ruthless enough to tell them."

Why did Malcolm Allison off-load you?

"Clash of personalities. I was a popular lad at Boro, as was Jim Platt. I don't rate him as a manager. He lived on the glory days of Joe Mercer. Mal was a good coach though. I don't agree with a man who can cut you to bits when he hasn't done what you've done; he wasn't a footballer. Jim and I were the only internationals at the club and he wanted rid of us. One of the things he said was that the club was trying to save money.

But then he employed a dance instructor called Lenny Hepple and a guy called Roger Spry who was a Karate black belt whose job it was to show us how to fall down and get back up again quickly. But when Heine Otto fell he damaged his shoulder and had to be taken to outpatients! Then to save money Allison told Harry the tea man that the club couldn't afford £18 a week to keep him. The players ended up paying Harry's wages just to keep him on.

I think one of the reasons for Stephen Bell's downfall was that Mal built him up too much. Stephen could have been a great footballer if he'd been taken in hand at seventeen but Mal let him get away with murder." [Stephen Bell was a teenage prodigy who played at sixteen but who discovered drink and women and was finished at twenty-two. Sadly he died in 2001]

Did he want you and Jim Platt out because you were established at the club? Maybe saw you as a threat to his authority?

"That's right. He wanted the kids to listen to him and nobody else - I don't even speak to him now. He let me go to Gillingham on a free."

Was that a good deal for you?

"It was a great deal for me. Keith Peacock took me down there and I was voted Third Division Player's Player of the Year. I was also voted the most popular ex-player in the history of Gillingham by the fans. They still ask me down there to play in charity games. It's tremendous. But if Mal had left and Willie Maddren had taken over while I was there, I'd loved to have stayed."

He probably would have been glad to have you. The club was in a terrible state when he took over as manager.

"He was on a hiding to nothing. If he'd had Steve Gibson behind him it may have been different!"

In your last year did it seem Boro were on the slide?

"As a player you don't notice. You just go in and do your job."

Did derby games mean as much to you as they did to the local lads in the team?

"Of course they did. I played with my heart on my sleeve. I never professed to be the best in the world, but I let the opposition know I was there. When I got the ball I went forward. Juninho did the same, but as we were saying, what you see all the time now is a player run twenty yards with the ball, then pass it twenty yards back.

When we beat Newcastle three-one in the Coca Cola Cup back in 1996, all three goals came from balls played in from wide positions. I think Boro need to change the way they play. The best ball for a centre-forward is the one that comes back from the by-line. That's the way forward."

Who was the best full-back you played against?

"Derek Statham, who played for West Brom was a good lad. The other one was Tony Dunne who played for Manchester United when they won the European Cup in 1968. He was finishing as I was starting, a very good player though. Kenny Sansom too; we had a go at each other for five or six years, the same with Frank Gray. One day you'd be on top, the next time it might be their turn but you'd have a go at them."

You must have come across a few who tried to break your legs.

"Yeah, there were a few. Les Strong at Fulham was a nasty piece of work. There were a few who didn't like me taking the piss out of them. They'd go for me rather than the ball. I was at Charlton one day and it turned out that Alf Ramsey was at the game. He asked if I was English! Raich Carter said in the 'paper, after I'd played at Hull for Burnley, that I reminded him of Stanley Matthews. I didn't realise he was a former Middlesbrough manager."

Did you feel part of the community when you played?

"Yeah, but I was a country lad. I was very overawed when I first came. I knew nothing about contracts. I would have signed for ten bob a week, never mind £200, as long as I could play football."

Having been sold to Gillingham, how did you end up back on Teesside?

"After Gillingham, I went to Dallas, Texas, on a six-month contract. Gordon Jago took me there. Then I came back to Millwall and played with Teddy Sheringham. After a few games for Millwall, I injured my Achilles tendon, which was nasty, so I came back up here to Hartlepool and played two games for them before pulling my hamstring. I thought then that it was time to get out. I didn't want to get typecast as a has-been, so I started to play Northern League."

Did you get a few kickings in the Northern League?

"Yeah, they were queuing up."

How long were you in the Northern League?

"I played for Billington Synthonia, ICI's work team for four years. I was player manager of South Bank, then player manager of Ferryhill. I seem to like lost causes. By that time I was playing sweeper, which I enjoyed."

Do you still play?

"I play a bit for Steve Gibson's team, Bulkhaul, on Sundays. I've been doing it for eleven or twelve years now. Bulkhaul go abroad every year to play, Steve took them to Cyprus this year for some games against the forces. I was coaching in America so I couldn't go."

Did you win all your caps with Boro?

"No, I got the first when I was a part-timer with Coleraine. I came on as sub against Norway. I got nineteen of my twenty-six caps with Boro, which makes me one of Boro's most capped players. People tend to forget, Wilf Mannion got twenty-six, Eric McMordie got twenty-one. I'm proud of that because not many players get a lot of caps playing for an unfashionable club."

It must have been heart-breaking to miss out on the 1982 World Cup with Northern Ireland?

"I was injured in France the month before. We got beat four-one in the Parc de Princes and I pulled a hamstring. The lads were very good about it. Billy Bingham gave me an extra two weeks to get fit, unfortunately I couldn't do it. But I got a postcard signed by all the lads. I sat in the Eston Institute bar watching the games. It broke my heart not to be there."

It must have been harder to take because Northern Ireland turned out to be one of the teams of the tournament.

"I more or less put them through. We played Portugal at Windsor Park. It was nil-nil with ten minutes left, I got the ball on the by-line, crossed it, and Gerry Armstrong scored. A lot of people said they wouldn't have got there but for me. But I got the same money as the lads who did go, which I thought was tremendous."

Playing International football must be a fantastic experience, but without being disrespectful, doesn't playing in front of 10,000 at Windsor Park take the gloss off it?

"The point is we're not a big country. We've got six counties; the Republic of Ireland has twenty-six. We've got to depend on people who play in the English League, and there aren't that many. Our best time was the eighties. Now we've got Gillespie, Lennon, and the boy Hughes at Wimbledon. We're lacking the quality of Jennings, McIlroy and Whiteside. The lads are trying their best but because the country is so small we're never going to qualify for every tournament."

Every few years someone says there should by an all-Ireland team. What do you think?

"I've had so many letters asking me about this but where will the games be played, North or South? How many players will there be from each? There wouldn't be many from the North. What sort of flag would they play under? We'd never agree. The Irish temperament is like that. The two governing bodies would never agree."

John Hendrie

Scottish forward, John Hendrie, made his name with Bradford, and was a key member of The Bantams' side which ran Boro so close in the 1987-88 play-offs. After short spells with Newcastle and Leeds, John signed for Boro in the summer of 1990. Early in his first season he scored probably the most famous goal seen at Ayresome Park. In a game against Millwall he picked up the ball deep in his own half, ran with it all the way to the Millwall box and scored. When Lennie Lawrence replaced Colin Todd in 1991, John Hendrie was a key member of the team. In the promotion season of 1991-1992, he was used mainly as a winger with Stuart Ripley on the other side to feed the strike force of Paul Wilkinson and Bernie Slaven. In the inaugural Premier League season 1992-1993 he was used more often as a striker alongside Wilkinson. The move paid off as he hit a hat-trick against Blackburn in front of the Match of the Day cameras in December 1992. Sadly he couldn't prevent Boro being relegated at the end of that season. When Bryan Robson replaced Lennie Lawrence in 1994 Hendrie was still first choice striker, and scored 15 goals as Boro were promoted back to the Premier League in 1994-95. He scored both goals as Boro defeated Luton two-one in the last League game at Ayresome Park in April 1995. Due to injuries, and big-name signings, Hendrie was never again a first choice at Boro. He left in 1996 to reform his partnership with Paul Wilkinson at Barnsley. He was named Player of the Year as The Tykes were promoted to the Premiership. After a short spell as Barnsley player-manager, he now works in the media.

How did you come to start your career at Coventry?
"Coventry were the first club that were interested in me. I played for a team in Scotland called Postle Park Y.M. Kenny Dalglish played for them and they were Coventry's nursery team. All the good boys from the age of fourteen would go down to Coventry on trial. From fourteen I used to go to Coventry every summer. They were the first team to give me a chance. I'm Celtic mad, they were my team as a boy, but Coventry had the best youth policy in the country at that time. I always had the belief that if I didn't make it in England I could go back to Scotland. Whereas Scottish lads are always trying to get a move to England."

Do you think that's why you've never been capped by Scotland?
"Yes. If I'd played in Scotland until I was twenty it would have been a different matter. I had a chance to join Aberdeen at one stage and if I'd done that I'm convinced I would have got a cap. It's because I've not kicked a ball in Scotland. I left school on a Friday afternoon and signed for Coventry that night. There are players I've played with, Darren Jackson, John Robertson, who couldn't get picked when we were at Newcastle, who've gone back to Scotland and got caps. Having said that I'm not moaning about it. I've no regrets about making my living South of the border. That's the only disappointing part, everything else has been great."

How did you come to sign for Bradford?
"I'd been given a free transfer by Coventry. Bobby Gould kicked me out. Gordon Milne signed me, Dave Sexton gave me my debut. Going to Bradford was a drop of two divisions, but I found my feet. I was good for Bradford, Bradford was good for me."

Did playing for Bradford on the day of the fire change the way you thought about the game?
"It put everything into perspective - football became secondary. Even now people ask questions and thinking back to that day numbs you. You are affected by the situation, you can't get away from it, especially after seeing some of the things I did that day. As a young lad at Coventry I was probably too intense about football taking it too seriously, but if you've been through a disaster like that, your attitude would be different."

When Bradford lost the promotion play-off at Ayresome Park, how big a blow was that?
"It was an almighty blow, because I'd had four years at Bradford. We'd done a lot in those four years, we'd grown up together, come through

the fire together. Even to this day I've still got an affinity with the club. You don't throw anything like that away. So it was a big disappointment. If we'd got promoted, I might have stayed there."

You must have fancied yourselves, having beaten Boro in the three previous games that season.

"Yes, we'd played particularly well against Boro. We didn't lose it at Ayresome Park, we lost it in the first leg when we absolutely battered the Boro. We won two-one but it should have been five or six. We lost the tie there. Boro had a second bite at the cherry when it should have been all over."

Of the two promotions you had at Boro, which did you enjoy most?

"The second one, because we'd been at the top all year and the club was a bit more high profile with Bryan Robson coming in. Plus the fact that I played down the middle which I prefer because you're more involved and you get more goals. In Lennie's promotion season he used myself and Stuart Ripley wide, so a lot of time I was doing the donkey work up and down the flank."

What was the reaction of the players when you found out that Bryan Robson was the new manager?

"Personally I was delighted, because I'd been at the club for four years and Lennie's final year had been a big disappointment. I was thinking to myself that I couldn't go through another season like that."

Playing in front of six thousand at Ayresome Park, things like that?

"Not just that, the club needed a big lift, I needed a lift. If an ordinary run of the mill manager had come in, it would have done nothing for me. I needed someone to give me a lift, and as it worked out it was a great season. Nigel Pearson was a big factor too - he's a good organiser. That's what we lacked the previous season, we had good players, but it's important you're organised."

Is there one game that stands out as the highlight of your career so far?

"I wouldn't say one, there's a few; the last game at Ayresome Park for instance, that was fantastic. The ground was red and white all over, we won two-one, and we knew more or less that we were up. Scoring the last goal there was special as well. That meant a lot to me. My mum and dad were in the stand, they didn't get down very often. The promotion game at Molineux in 1992 was a fantastic day as well. Scoring a hat-trick against Blackburn and Kenny Dalglish, my boyhood hero, I've been fortunate that I've got quite a few rather than just one."

Would you have swapped all the ups and downs for ten years at a mid table Premiership team?

"No, not at all. I've had more highs than lows, but I prefer exciting times, even if you're battling against relegation. There's nothing like winning things, and having won promotion and First Division titles, there's nothing like it."

Having played for Leeds and Newcastle, do you think Boro can be as big as those two clubs if they get things right on the pitch?

"Potentially yes, but maybe not as big as Newcastle - they're talking about a 70,000 seater stadium! I'm not saying Boro couldn't get those crowds one day, but I certainly think Boro are bigger than Leeds already."

How do the fans of the three clubs compare?

"I think it's all about whether you're successful or not. If you are doing well you always get on better with the fans. If you've had a bad time you don't have the same affinity."

You've got a reputation as a joker in the dressing room, is that justified do you think?

"I think it's important that you have the banter in the dressing room, that helps build team spirit. If I'm quiet and subdued, I feel that might affect the other players. If I'm bubbly and enjoying myself that will boost morale. But if you play jokes you're expected to take them, and I take them."

What's the worst thing you've had done to you?

"My eyebrows by far [laughs], although I got my backside burned when we went to Portugal after promotion. I fell asleep sunbathing and the lads pulled my shorts down, but you can cover your backside. If your eyebrows are done you have to face the world without any eyebrows. [Laughs]"

How did that happen?

"Me and Jamie Pollock had a stupid game. I forget what we were drinking but we both had clear drinks, unbeknown to me Jamie's was water. I'd been stitched up by the rest of the lads. I went to bed pie-eyed and woke up with one eyebrow. So I thought bugger it and shaved the other one off myself. It's important you take those things well, I didn't react in a negative way."

Is it a regret that you didn't have more chances to play with Juninho?

"I would have liked to have played more with him. It's not a regret, it's just one of those things. That's up to the manager. He didn't give me the opportunity as often as I would have liked, but I've no sour grapes about that. I played a few games at the back-end of Juninho's first season, but I'd had a nightmare with injuries that year. I played against Forest at home, Villa away and Leeds away. I thought I performed well. That was the last time I played with him, apart from pre-season games and games abroad, like in Bangkok in 1996."

When you left was it the club's decision to sell you, rather than you wanting to go?

"One hundred per cent, there's no doubt about that. My contract was up after spending six and a half years at the club. Financially it would have been better for me to wait for my contract to expire because I would have got a free transfer, and clubs wouldn't have had to pay a fee – I could have got a better deal. Bryan Robson pulled me in after we got back from Bangkok and told me there was a £250,000 offer from Barnsley. I hadn't caused any rumblings, I didn't have a pet lip because I wasn't playing. I'd been on the bench every game and Robbo kept me involved all the time. I'd had six great years at Middlesbrough, I was going into my last year to enjoy it, and at my age it was great being involved at the club with Emerson, Juninho and Ravanelli. There's no way I was looking to move. Robbo told me he couldn't give me a two-year contract, which is what Barnsley offered. Plus the fact that he wouldn't have got any money for me if I'd gone at the end of the season. He thought it was worth my while to talk to them. I would gladly have stayed, even though I wasn't playing I wasn't unhappy, I love the club. When I left The Riverside for the last time there was a lump in my throat. The hardest part about leaving the club wasn't getting used to Barnsley, it was forgetting Middlesbrough after being at the club for so long. You've got to realise as well, Branco was paid fortunes for eight months football, I'd been there six and a bit years, the club paid £500,000 for me, and got £250,000 back, so I didn't feel they were doing me any favours. Robbo said they'd give me part of that fee, so in effect they were paying me to go, which is even more of a push out of the door!"

The writing's on the wall then.

"Of course it is. I had to go and think about the situation, i.e. that Barnsley's close to where I live, I wouldn't need to move house, I've got another two year's security, and I had a better chance of first team football. Wilko told me they had a chance of promotion, so I decided to give it a go. But I certainly didn't want to go."

What was your best goal?

"Millwall. I've scored a few spectacular long shots, but that's one I'll never forget. It won Goal of the Season for the Tyne Tees region that year.

John Hendrie's bulldog spirit wins him the ball against Brighton

Anyone can score long-range shots, but it's not very often you get the ball on the edge of your own box, take it right to the other end and score."

If you could change one thing in your career what would it be?
" I'd be six foot four, run like Linford Christie and head like Joe Jordan. [Laughs]... It's hard to say, I'm not one to cry over spilt milk. I think you make your decisions and you get on with it. You never say I should have done this or that, because that's negative thinking. It goes back to the point about being bubbly in the dressing room. I think of that as one of my assets and I think that's infectious to other people, which is important. My belief is that you've got to be positive in everything."

The longest spells of your career are four years at Bradford, and six at Boro. Both sets of fans still have a great affinity with you. Are you proud of that?
"Without a doubt, at Coventry I was learning my trade. I was only at Newcastle and Leeds for a season, so it wasn't like Bradford and Boro where I was part of things for longer. I still go and watch Bradford whenever I can; same with Boro. I was at the Old Trafford Semi-Final, both Coca Cola Cup Finals, and the F.A. Cup Final, so I'm prepared to give my weekends up to follow them. I've got a feeling for that club, I want them to do really well. The same with Bradford, I was desperate for them to stay up when they were in The Premiership. So it does give me pride that I'm well thought of because I think the world of them."

Juninho

Juninho is arguably the best player ever to wear the red shirt. Fans of the late Wilf Mannion may disagree, but in modern times it's difficult to think of anyone who compares. He arrived in England as part of the Brazil team which beat England three-one at Wembley in 1995. He signed for Boro in a blaze of publicity, not all of it favourable, and made his debut against Leeds at the Riverside in November 1995. His slide rule pass to Jan Aage Fjortoft set up Boro's goal after ten minutes, in a game which finished one-one. He spent the remainder of that season acclimatising to England and the Premiership as Boro finished mid-table in their first season back in the Premiership. 1996-97 was of course the season of three points docked, two cup finals, and relegation. In the midst of all this Juninho produced the form of his life. His commitment to the cause was second only to the quality of his play, his tears following relegation at Elland Road produced one of the images of the season. Only Gianfranco Zola prevented Juninho winning the Premiership Player of the Year award. Following relegation, Athletico Madrid paid £12m and he went to Spain to safeguard his position in the Brazil team for the 1998 World Cup. Following a brilliant start to the season he suffered a broken ankle which ruled him out of the 1998 World Cup. This effectively ended his career with Madrid. A return to Boro on loan in 1999 was a disappointment, as he struggled to regain his best form in a team which was itself struggling. A move back to Brazil helped him find his form, and regain his place in the Brazil team in time for the 2002 World Cup. Following Brazil's victory he re-signed for Boro, only to suffer a knee ligament injury in pre-season, which ruled him out until March. The start of the 2003-04 season saw him fit ready and hoping to return to the form of 1996-97.

You came to notice when you scored in Brazil's three-one win over England at Wembley in 1995. Was that the point when European clubs started to take an interest in you?

"Nobody knows you before you play for the national team. People here don't know many players in Brazil. When we came here it was an opportunity to introduce our team to the people in England. The first club that came to me was Middlesbrough. They showed more interest than others. I didn't know if there were many clubs interested, I only knew Middlesbrough were. Bryan Robson and Keith Lamb [Chief Executive] came to Brazil, and at that time my contract with Sao Paolo was finished, so we had a deal."

Is it true that Arsenal tried to hijack the deal at the last minute?

"Yes, somebody told me to wait one more day, because Arsenal were interested. But I didn't know anyone from Arsenal, nobody talked to me, except an agent. I nearly had the deal with Middlesbrough; I couldn't turn round and say I was waiting for Arsenal, because the deal was close. So I didn't wait, and signed for Middlesbrough."

When you signed for the club the area got a lot of bad publicity in the national newspapers. Were you aware of that at the time?

"I just looked at the football. The ambition of the club at that time, they expected to play in Europe. I watched a lot of English football and liked the style of play. When I came I was thinking about playing and adapting to English football as soon as possible."

How does English football compare to Brazilian football?

"It's a lot different, first of all the condition of the pitch is totally different. In Brazil you need three or four touches to control the ball. Here all the pitches are fabulous. That makes the game a lot quicker than in Brazil. The weather is different too. In Brazil you sometimes play when the temperature is forty degrees. That makes the game a bit slower, because it's impossible to run when it's forty degrees. Here, the weather helps makes the game faster. You don't get tired early in the game so it's easier to play for ninety minutes. In Brazil also it's a bit more tactical. When you are in front you sit back and mark. In England that doesn't happen, if you score one you try to score two or three. That gives opportunities for the opposition to score too. So it's a very open game here."

What was the hardest thing to become accustomed to when you arrived?

"I think it was the weather. I came in October I think, and it was beginning to get very cold. I really felt the difference. My lips got chapped, I had to wear hats to train, things like that."

You'll always be associated with 1996-1997. When you think about that season, is it with pride in your own performances and the fact that the club came so close, or is the disappointment of losing Cup Finals and relegation the overriding memory?

"It was a very strange season because sometimes we were so confident at home. But when we went away there were a lot of mistakes, and early in some matches we were often one or two nil down. So it was hard to get results when we played away. We knew we were a good team, that's why we got to two Cup Finals. We didn't deserve to go down. We obviously also had the problem with the FA and the three point deduction. So there were problems in that season but people still say that was the most exciting season we've had because of the quality of the football."

Was it a problem that you played so well that season, that every-thing went through you, so if the opposition stopped you they stopped the team; maybe you took on too much responsibility?

"Maybe, because we went well in the cups which were one off games. You win and you're through, lose and you go out. I think we had more concentration in those games than in the league. If we lost in the league we'd think we have however many games left to get away from the bottom. The concentration wasn't the same in the league as the cup games. Maybe that's why we went down."

People still talk about the Chelsea game as the best individual per-formance they've seen. Is it one that stands out in your memory? [Boro 1 Chelsea 0, 22nd March 1997. Juninho dominated the entire match and scored the only goal with a diving header, in a must win game.]

"I remember it because it was a real important game for us to win if we wanted to stay up. We needed a result, and Chelsea were a great team. I had the opportunity to score, and we got the three points. That was the most important thing. That's why people talk about that game, if we'd lost, maybe we would have lost the opportunity to stay up."

After relegation you went to Atletico Madrid and played well until your broken ankle. After that you seemed to have problems at the club.

"I'd never had a bad injury before. When you come back from a bad knock you need support from people around you; the manager, and the club because you need time to come back to your best. When I was injured the club changed managers. [Raddy Antic was replaced by former Italian national coach Arrigo Sacchi.] That was the start of my problems. First of all he wanted to play me in a different position, and I wasn't doing well because I had lost confidence. Nobody supported me to help me get it

1997 – Juninho celebrates his goal against Chelsea as the Boro fans go wild

back. I stayed nearly two years with those problems, until I went to Brazil to get my football back."

Arrigo Sacchi always plays 4-4-2. Was the problem that he was trying to fit you into a rigid formation?

"He wanted me to play as a striker, with my back to the defender. That's not my style of play so it was difficult to play that role well. I wasn't playing well, so they bought another guy to play up front, who was a striker. So of course he played better than me.

After Sacchi left, Claudio Ranieri came, and he's from the same school. So I was upset with Atletico Madrid at that time because they never thought of the players they had. The new manager would bring five or six players in, and they forgot about the players who were already there. So I didn't get the support from the club. That's why I wanted to leave."

So you came back to Boro in 1999.

"It wasn't a very good idea to come back. When you're on loan people don't treat you the same as when you're permanent at the club. I didn't find a good atmosphere in my second spell here.

I should have gone to Brazil then because the support would have been there from my family. I lost maybe a year when I should have gone to Brazil to get my football back."

You got back into the Brazil team before the 2002 World Cup. Before the tournament there was criticism of the team in Brazil. Is that a problem that you are always compared to the teams of 1970 and 1982?

"There was a lot of criticism because we didn't play well in qualifying for the World Cup. But not because we were too defensive. In the World Cup we played with one up front, but we played myself, Ronaldo, Rivaldo, and Ronaldinho; all attacking players. We weren't defensive in the World Cup; we scored a lot of goals. But when you play in the South American qualifiers you have to travel ten or eleven hours, train one or two days, then go to play. Sometimes you can't maintain your level of performance, due to the travelling, the pitches are different, the way you play is different. The players think all the World Cup qualifiers should be played at the same time."

This is probably an impossible question to answer properly, but can you tell me what it feels like to play in a World Cup Final?

"It's marvellous because it's every player's dream to play in a World Cup. We all imagine playing in the final and winning the title. It was my dream when I was a kid. In the beginning you dream about becoming a footballer. When you are a footballer, you dream of playing with the

2002 — Denilson and Juninho celebrate winning Brazil's fifth World Cup crown

national team, and winning things with the national team. That's what's happened with me. I always say nothing in football compares. I've never played in the Champions League but, I'm sure it's not the same as playing in a World Cup, because you know people all over the world are watching you. It was incredible, but when you're there you don't think about that. You only think about playing like a normal game. When you relax after the game you think about how far you've been. Before you only think about playing."

You've got fifty caps for Brazil and a World Cup Winners' medal. What is there left for you to achieve in football?

"Winning titles. Middlesbrough is the club which has given me more support than any other, and I still have a job to do here. Middlesbrough has to become a medium to big club. We've brought international players in, we have a good squad, and we have to fight for some titles or fight to go to Europe."

In your three spells here who have you most enjoyed playing with?

"I had a good link with Ravanelli, and with Emerson there was support behind me, so when I had the ball I could look forward and use Ravenelli's movement. We understood each other. When I played with Atletico in the beginning (Christian) Vieri was there, and we also had a good understanding."

How are you enjoying being a father?

"Outside football, it's the most exciting experience I've had. We're expecting our third. It's good to build a family."

Did that help you when you had the long injury lay off last season?

"Yes, it helped me a lot. They always supported me. When you go home and your children smile for you, and want to play with you, you forget what you are upset about."

TEES-SIDE

Juninho Boro/Brazil Flag £14.99

Cameroon Boro Flag £14.99

Juninho Legend £14.99

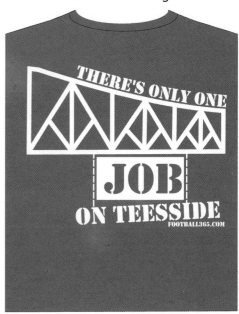

There's Only One Job On Teesside £14.